Preface

Many factors contribute to successful performances in sport. In addition to the physical, technical and strategic demands of sport, performers must be able to remain focused, maintain emotional control, sustain self-confidence and constantly apply themselves in both training and competition. In your own sport, you will undoubtedly be able to recognise the mental demands placed on performers. Meeting these demands may be relatively easy when things are going well but less so during times of difficulty (eg poor form, distractions, injury). Coaches typically identify a range of mental qualities that seem to underpin successful sports performance – qualities encompassed in the four Cs: commitment, confidence, concentration and control.

Participation in competitive sport can be a stressful experience inducing strong emotions such as anxiety, frustration, aggression and elation. While these emotions may have both a positive or negative effect on performance, it is essentially the ability to control and channel such emotions that is crucial to success in sport. This exciting new booklet, *Handling Pressure,* will help coaches and performers control negative thoughts and feelings, and channel positive emotions to produce an appropriate state of activation or readiness in both mind and body to promote optimal performance. It includes a wealth of ideas that can readily be used by coaches and integrated into their everyday coaching practice without making substantial changes to existing sessions and programmes.

Advice is offered on how to learn and use various coping strategies including physically-related stress management techniques (eg rhythmic breathing, centring, progressive muscle relaxation and physical activation) and mental techniques (eg meditative relaxation, imagery-based relaxation, cognitive restructuring and mental activation). In addition, there are programmes on attitude management and contingency planning. All these programmes will help your performers develop integrated coping responses to the stress of competition. The maintenance of appropriate mental and physical states prior to and during sports performance can only serve to increase the probability of short- and long-term success.

The pack is divided into two parts:

Part One, written in home study format, contains two chapters and provides an overview of mental training, an insight into the concepts of stress and anxiety, followed by an introduction to the relevant stress management techniques and coping strategies. These chapters will help you to:

- identify the contribution of the fundamental mental skills to overall sports performance
- assess your knowledge of basic mental training methods
- identify and explain the process by which performers experience stress and anxiety
- describe the importance of coping strategies in managing the pressures of competition in your sport.

Part Two consists of seven practical mental training programmes – many involve working directly with your performers either within or outside your normal coaching sessions. Following a session on performance profiling and assessment, these practical sessions will help you develop ways of controlling negative emotions and activating optimal states by applying:

- physical relaxation and activation techniques
- mental relaxation and activation techniques
- cognitive restructuring and attitude management techniques
- contingency planning techniques.

By working through the programmes with your performers, you should be able to identify:

- the mental skills they require to manage stress and handle pressure effectively
- how mental training can be incorporated into the overall training programmes
- coping strategies to eliminate negative thoughts and feelings as well as strengthen and maintain positive emotional states.

A final summary with follow-up references concludes the pack. This is an essential pack for coaches and performers looking for the competitive edge – it may also be of benefit to sport psychologists, team managers and support staff.

The following icons are used in the pack:

Key to symbols used in the text:

  An activity

  Approximate length of time to be spent on the activity

  Audiotape

  Benefits

Throughout this pack, the pronouns he, she, him, her and so on are interchangeable and intended to be inclusive of both men and women. It is important in sport, as elsewhere, that men and women have equal status and opportunities.

Contents

PART ONE

Chapter One: Overview of Mental Training

1.0 What's in It for You?

The field of mental training is still relatively new to many coaches, although the importance of the mind in sport has been recognised for many years. Successful performance rests on the effective integration and execution of physical and mental skills. Therefore, without developing mental qualities such as confidence, commitment, concentration and control (the 4Cs), peak performance will remain an unattainable dream for most performers.

Before examining in greater detail methods of handling the pressure commonly associated with sports competition, it is important to consider the effect of mental factors on performance and help you assess your experience and knowledge in the use of mental training techniques and strategies. This chapter provides an overview of mental training and by the end, you should be able to:

- identify the contribution of the fundamental mental qualities (the 4Cs) to overall sports performance in your sport

- assess your knowledge and experience of basic mental training methods

- communicate to your performers the value of mental practice to improve their sports performance.

1.1 Importance of Mental Qualities

You are probably already aware of the influence of mental factors on sports performance – in learning new skills as well as in producing consistent high level performance. As a coach, you inherently know the type of performer you would put your money on to win when the going gets tough. They are the performers who probably:

- show greater control over their emotions and know how to channel them effectively

- remain intrinsically dedicated to their sport and totally committed to a tough training regime

- maintain concentration on what is relevant to peak performance and tune out distractions

- display a confident image and physical presence whether they are winning or losing.

These are all signs, both in training and competition, which are indicative of an individual or team performer who can handle the pressure of competition effectively. The first activity will help you consider the impact of mental factors or qualities on your performers in more detail.

ACTIVITY I

1. Reflect on a recent coaching session or competition in which one of your performers:

   - performed well beyond expectation
   - significantly underachieved.

2. List all the reasons why you felt the performer over or underachieved:

Overachieved because:	Underachieved because:

3   List any mental factors or qualities you believe might have contributed to the over or underachievement or subsequent mental state:

4   Identify the key situations in your sport when these factors might be important (eg at the start, at a penalty, following an injury):

Now turn over.

2   *Some of the reasons listed to explain over or underachievement might have included the following:*

Overachieved because:	Underachieved because:
Stuck to agreed game plan	Lack of fitness
Good mental and physical preparation	Poor weather conditions or facilities
Maintained focus and emotional control	Unfavourable officiating decisions
Selected appropriate equipment (eg type of club, racing tyres)	Injury or fear of injury
Ideal conditions (eg no wind, dry pitch)	Strength of opponent
Adapted to changing circumstances (eg score line, opponent's tactics)	Breakdown in skills
High confidence due to good fitness level	Poor tactical decisions
	Failed to cope with the pressure – choked at a critical point
	Distracted (eg by crowd, officials, opponent, incident)
	Failure by other team members

3   *The sort of mental factors or qualities you may have listed could probably be summarised under the 4Cs:*

-   *Commitment – will to win, dedication, desire*
-   *Control of emotions – for example of anxiety, anger, frustration*
-   *Concentration – quality of focus or attention*
-   *Confidence – positive attitude, self-belief in abilities.*

4   *Consider your answers by reviewing the following specific situations that in some sports might make significant demands on mental qualities:*

-   *At the start of a race, game or event.*
-   *At the end of a race, last ten minutes of a game, final event (eg last jump, last piece of apparatus, end of a set, approaching match point).*
-   *Following a foul, an unfavourable officiating decision, an injury, equipment failure.*
-   *Before a difficult or particularly crucial situation (eg the jump following a no-jump, the most difficult piece of apparatus, at a penalty/short corner, in extra time, at a scrum close to your own try line, break point down at 3-3).*

You will probably have recognised that mental factors contribute significantly to performance in your sport[1]. To illustrate the potential significance of these mental qualities, read the following example from tennis.

Sampras versus Moya, Australian Open 1997

Total play time:	87 minutes
Action time:	17 minutes
Time between action:	70 minutes (potential thinking time)

During these 70 minutes, there was the opportunity for both negative and positive thoughts, feelings and self-talk; plenty of time to think oneself into or out of the match.

---

1   If you need further guidance in identifying the contribution of mental factors to your sport, you are recommended to *Mental Skills: an introduction for sports coaches,* available from Coachwise Ltd (0113 231 1310).

1.2　Mental Training Techniques

Most competitors use a variety of mental techniques – often as a result of experience or trial-and-error rather than through teaching. They have learnt ways (strategies) to help them cope with difficult situations both in a sports context and perhaps in life more generally (eg dealing with examinations, interviews, work pressures, relationships). Coaches can accelerate and enhance this process by introducing and systematically developing appropriate techniques for specific occasions. You may already use or be familiar with a number of these techniques. Try Activity 2.

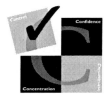

ACTIVITY 2

1 List any mental techniques you or your performers use (with or without your input) or may wish to use to improve the mental qualities listed in the left-hand column. An example technique for each quality is given to help you:

Qualities	Techniques
Commitment	*Goal-setting*
Concentration	*Imagery*
Confidence	*Positive thinking*
Control	*Relaxation training*

2 Describe in more detail the techniques you have listed under **control**:

Now turn over.

1   *Table 1 provides an overview of the sort of techniques that can be used to strengthen each quality:*

Qualities	Techniques
Commitment	Goal-setting Refocusing Positive thinking (eg use of positive statements)
Concentration	Imagery Distraction training Developing routines and using crib cards Segmenting performance into easy-to-manage components Simulated competition training
Confidence	Positive self-talk statements Imagery Goal-setting Routines Cognitive restructuring (positive thinking) Simulated competition training
Control	Relaxation training Breathing exercises (eg centring) Cognitive restructuring Positive self-statements Developing routines Simulated competition training Attitude management What ifs? Contingency planning Mental/physical activation training

Table 1: Overview of mental qualities and techniques

2   *Many of the techniques listed under* **control** *will be the focus of subsequent programmes in this pack. You should note that the techniques in this category also tend to appear elsewhere. This demonstrates the versatility of these techniques and the way in which they can be integrated into an overall mental training strategy.*

If you had any difficulty with this activity or if any of the techniques are new to you, you may find it useful to develop your understanding further before continuing with this pack. You are recommended to the NCF home study pack *Mental Skills: an introduction for sports coaches* as well as other mental skills packs, available from Coachwise Ltd (0113 231 1310).

1.3 Learning Mental Techniques

Whatever techniques (mental, technical, physical) you wish your performers to develop, the cyclical process through which they learn, practise and apply these remains much the same:

STEP 1 Identify all the personal factors[1] that can positively affect performance. For each performer, you may wish to profile these factors using the following categories: technical, tactical, physical, mental qualities. Alternatively you might choose to take a *whole performer approach* (ie profile your performer's strengths and weaknesses on those factors deemed most important).

STEP 2 Identify with performers, their strengths and weaknesses in relation to each factor (Programme One, Page 58).

STEP 3 From this profiling, you will be able to determine with each performer the key factors that will result in the most profound improvements in performance. For example, the key factor might be greater emotional control, improved power, better decision-making. You may then identify critical times in training and competition when each of these becomes a major influence on performance.

STEP 4 Select the most appropriate way to make this improvement – this means you need to know the range of techniques possible and how to use them effectively.

STEP 5 Determine when the technique should be introduced into training, practice and eventually competition (see Section 1.4, Page 12). For some mental techniques such as imagery, there is also the question of when the technique can be used – before, during and after the session or competition.

STEP 6 Practise the technique – probably first in training and mock competitions. After a suitable period of time, monitor and assess the effectiveness of the technique. This can involve re-profiling your performer to check for relative improvements. If necessary, the performer may persist with this technique or use an alternative from the range available.

STEP 7 Apply and use the technique in actual competition – this should be done gradually and monitored carefully; start in less important competitions and progress to the more important ones.

NB Mental techniques, like physical ones, take time to learn, practise and use successfully – be patient and build them slowly.

---

1   These factors are often referred to as **qualities** in the performance profiling literature.

While many performers might recognise the impact of improved technical skills and fitness on sport success, some may be more reluctant to acknowledge the need to commit time and effort to the development of mental qualities. You may need, therefore, to discuss the potential value of mental training with your performers, so they appreciate what you are trying to achieve and how it will improve performance. This enhanced sense of ownership will increase their commitment and adherence to mental training. How and when you do this will depend very much on the performer – his profile, expectations and goals, and the overall training programme.

At what point in the training and competition calendar should you start to introduce new mental techniques? This will depend on a number of factors such as the following:

- Your performers' needs and goals, their relative importance of mental skills work to other aspects of training and their current use of mental techniques.

- The stage in the training cycle – new mental techniques should normally be introduced in the off-season, pre-season or early phase of the annual programme – not when they are undergoing new or particularly heavy training loads or in the major competition phase.

- Your availability of time – it is best to introduce new mental techniques when you have time to talk them through thoroughly with your performers.

ACTIVITY 3

1 Determine when you intend to introduce new mental techniques into the training programme for your performer (NB It may be helpful to select one or two performers now with whom you might work as you read through this pack). It may help first to identify the most important competitions and any periodization into pre-season training, preparation and recovery phases. Mark all these points on the table below and then determine the best time to introduce new mental skills work.

Month	Week 1	Week 2	Week 3	Week 4
Jan				
Feb				
Mar				
Apr				
May				
Jun				
Jul				
Aug				
Sep				
Oct				
Nov				
Dec				

2 Explain your decision:

Now turn over.

It is generally best to use the off-season or early training preparation phase to introduce or develop mental techniques. This ensures there is time to learn these new techniques and gradually apply them in training before using them in competitions.

1.4 Stress, Anxiety, Arousal and Activation in Sport

Over the years, there has been a great deal of confusion among both sport psychologists and coaches about the relationship between stress and performance, and how emotions such as anxiety fit into the picture. This is mainly because terms such as stress, anxiety, activation and arousal are often used interchangeably and, as a result, incorrectly. The following model (Figure 1) attempts to clarify the process of how stress may impact on performance in a way which integrates the role of activation, anxiety and arousal. Explaining this model should provide you with a convincing insight into a performer's experience of stress and its associated effects. This will then help you understand and identify with the specific stress management techniques introduced in Chapter Two and developed through the programmes in Part Two. It is useful to start with a definition of activation because it is ultimately the quality of the activation states which determine the quality of performance. It is then easier to see how stress (or stressors) can have a positive or negative effect on activation states.

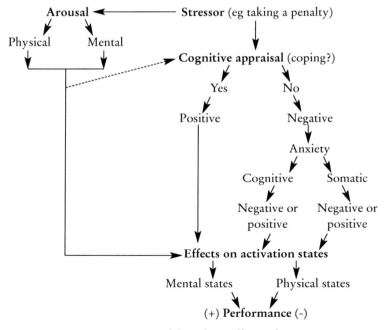

Figure 1: Model to show effects of stress

Activation

Activation refers to your mental and physical state as a total system. For optimal performance, it is necessary to generate an appropriate state of activation or readiness in both the mind and body – an ideal mental and physical performance state (often referred to as the ideal performance state or IPS). Physical activation reflects the functioning of several sub-systems (eg heart rate, blood pressure, body temperature, adrenalin levels and muscle tension). Similarly the mental state is affected by sub-systems such as the level of alertness, the quality and quantity of attention, the amount of interest or importance invested in the forthcoming activity. Different sports and activities require differing activation levels and may make specific demands on one or more of these sub-systems. For optimal performance therefore, there needs to be a match between your activation state and the demands of the activity you are about to perform. The following examples will make this clear.

Consider a gymnast competing on the beam who needs a relaxed focus to perform each move to maintain balance and remain on the beam throughout her event. A moderately intense physical state may be matched with a low intensity of mental activation.

The same gymnast competing in the floor exercise may need an elevated physical activation level to throw some of the tumbling routine skills that require more power and speed. In either case, the gymnast must know her ideal activation state for  each event because the task demands associated with the two events differ.

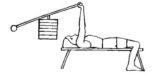

Similar differences exist for golfers who stand over a short putt for par to win a tournament and the activation level needed to play a mid-field position in football.

Consider the mental and physical activation state you would try to induce if asked to bench press 100kg. What if instead of bench pressing, you were suddenly asked to sink a five foot putt[1]? You would probably have to change both mental and physical activation levels to be successful.

---

1   This example was drawn from work by Hardy, Jones & Gould, 1996.

Ideal activation states are highly individual – some perform better when highly activated in both physical and mental terms; others function more effectively under lower levels of activation. Activation is two-dimensional (mental and physical) and refers simply to the state you are in at a given point in time. The goal for performers is to be able to find, regain or maintain their IPS (mental and physical states which are ideal to them) for the specific sport task at hand. Mental techniques that can produce consistently optimal activation levels are a priority.

Stress

Stress is best described as a process initiated when the brain interprets some internal or external stimulus (stressor) as potentially threatening to the individual – physically or psychologically damaging. Stressors also act as arousing agents which are responsible for causing mental and physiological **arousal** within the performer. In everyday life, for example, imagine the smell of beautiful perfume, the taste of a favourite food, starting a car in gear and it jerking forward or something simple like going for a run.

All these are external stimuli picked up by the senses, which can result in both mental (eg increased alertness) and/or physiological arousal (eg increased heart rate). In the sport context, internal stressors may include perceiving a lack of form due to injury or poor recent performances. The more common external/situational stressors include situations such as:

- competing at an important event for the first time
- playing in front of a particular individual or large crowd
- taking a penalty with one minute remaining
- arriving late to a competition and having too little time for a full personal warm-up.

The mind, at both a conscious and subconscious level, takes in all kinds of stimuli (stressors) all day long (eg extremes of noise, light) but it is how the stressor is perceived and appraised by the brain that is the key issue.

Cognitive appraisal

The second stage of the stress process involves appraising the demands imposed on the performer by the stressor. The brain does this so quickly that performers may not always be conscious of the process. The appraisal consists of two potentially subconscious questions:

- Is this stressor a potential threat – for example to my self-image or esteem?
- Do I have the personal resources to cope with the stressor?

If there is no perceived threat or the individual feels he has the resources to handle the stressor, there will be no negative mental and physical response. Accordingly, the large or small amounts of arousal associated with the stressor are viewed either neutrally or perhaps even as a positive influence on the activation states. In such cases, the individual is coping with the stressor and perceiving little stress. You may well know some performers who remain in control and positively aroused during what might be considered to be highly stressful situations. From their point of view (even subconsciously), they may not perceive any stressor, view the stressor as a challenge as opposed to a threat, or feel they have adequate resources (eg skills) to deal with the stressor (situation). This is where an important quality like self-confidence fits into the equation.

More often, however, the stressor is viewed as a threat and the individual perceives the personal resources to respond to such a threat are lacking or at least questionable. In this situation, the individual will probably perceive the symptoms of mental and particularly physiological arousal to be a little unpleasant (eg butterflies). In psychological terms, there is a perceived imbalance between the perceived demands imposed by the stressor (eg the need to score the penalty for personal and team reasons) and the perceived ability to meet such a demand (eg to score the penalty). In a typical case like this, the performer's system is under strain and the ensuing response experienced by the performer is anxiety.

Anxiety

The negative pathway described by the stress process culminates in anxiety which is why psychologists generally refer to it as the cognitive and physiological manifestation of stress. It is important to note that anxiety is represented by both cognitive (mental) and physical states:

- **Cognitive anxiety** is the mental component of anxiety characterised by fear of failure and negative expectations about performance[1]. In other words, when you worry or have negative thoughts and self-doubts about the task, you are experiencing cognitive anxiety.

- **Somatic anxiety** is the physical component of anxiety characterised by the performer's negative perception of her physiological state (arousal level). Somatic anxiety, therefore, is represented by the negatively perceived symptoms of nervousness, muscle tension, butterflies and increased heart rate and respiration.

1   Explanations based on work by Hardy et al, 1996.

Effects on performance

It is critical for coaches to understand the stress process. If mental and physical activation levels are the key determinants of performance, the consequences of the stress process on activation states are significant. Increased levels of mental and physical arousal occurring as a result of a stressor can have potentially positive effects on performance by elevating existing activation levels to a more appropriate level for the task at hand (see Section 2.5, Page 51). However, negatively perceived arousal in the form of cognitive and somatic anxiety can have detrimental effects on performance due to their direct effects on the activation state.

Many sport psychology theories have been proposed to try to explain the relationship between anxiety and performance. It is generally agreed that the relationship is complex – remember different skills within a sport sometimes require different levels of mental and physical activation (eg a running passing shot in tennis might require a higher level of activation than executing a delicate drop volley; lifting a heavy weight would require a higher level of activation than shooting at a target). In some situations, the level of anxiety (cognitive or somatic) therefore might enhance the performance because it raises activation to an optimal level.

Some argue that stress has a positive effect because it challenges the performer and induces learning and personal growth. After all, the mind is like a muscle – if you want to make it stronger, you have to work it and expose it to different resistances. Research suggests that a number of elite performers actually perceive anxiety to have a positive effect on performance, even though in reality it is a negative mental and emotional state. What the brain subconsciously perceives as negative, the performer may consciously perceive as positive. This is an important point because coaches will work with both types of performers – those who like to be mentally and/or physically highly activated and enjoy some anxiety and those who cannot cope with the effects of either high anxiety or a high activation level.

The real issue in this pack, therefore, is about understanding individual and sport-specific requirements and perceptions. It is less about supporting general laws about how anxiety affects performance. Coaches should focus on:

- identifying the optimal activation states, bearing in mind the demands of the sport and the preference of the performer
- the fact that anxiety and arousal can influence activation states both positively and negatively
- teaching techniques to performers which will serve to trigger, control or regain optimal activation.

To explore this process yourself, try the following activity.

ACTIVITY 4

1   Describe what you perceive to be the optimal mental and physical activation
    level or state for your sport:

Mental	Physical

2   List some examples of stressful situations that performers would typically
    encounter in your sport:

Continued...

3　Using one example, reflect on an occasion when you or your performer experienced the stressor but handled it effectively and performed well (eg things seemed within control, everything came together, coped with every situation). What did you notice about your feelings, thoughts, attentional focus? Did these differ from the characteristics of your optimal activation states described in Question 1?

- Occasion (eg a particular competition):

- Thoughts, feelings, attentional focus (eg aroused, energised, mentally alert but perhaps nervous):

- Differences between this and the optimal activation state described in Question 1:

4　Repeat this exercise but this time reflect on an experience where you or one of your performers did not handle the stressor and performance suffered as a result.

- Occasion (eg a particular competition):

- Thoughts, feelings, attentional focus (eg too tense, negative doubts, stiff, froze, choked):

- Differences between this and the optimal activation state described in Question 1:

5 Symptoms of anxiety may have featured in both good and poor performances. Describe, in as much detail as possible, what you think the positive and negative effects of both cognitive and somatic anxiety are on performance in your sport:

	Positive	Negative
Cognitive		
Somatic		

Now turn over.

1 *The descriptors of optimal states of mental and physical activation are unique to the individual but might include some or more of the following:*

Optimal Mental Preparation	Optimal Physical Activation
Positive/enthusiastic	Mild butterflies
Confident	Elevated heart rate
Appropriately focused	Slightly increased sweating
Excited	Rhythmic breathing
Alert	Calmness
Fully committed	A sense of high energy and readiness
Interested	

2 *Compare your answers with the following examples of situations that might be perceived as stressful:*

- *Trials where selection is taking place.*
- *Taking a penalty on which the outcome of the match is likely to rest.*
- *Performing in front of a large or hostile crowd, large TV audience.*
- *When performing poorly or being heavily beaten.*
- *Repeated unfavourable or inconsistent officiating decisions.*
- *After an error which could prove very costly.*
- *When very tired.*
- *When losing to lower ranked opposition.*
- *The period immediately before the start of the competition.*

3/4   *Compare your answers with the following table:*

	Performed Well Under Stress	*Performed Poorly Under Stress*
Thoughts	Viewed every set-back as a challenge	No positive response I could recall
	Slipped into a natural routine	Disorganised thinking, disrupted routine
	Rehearsed game plan	Over-analysed game plan
	Positive mental rehearsal	Imagined failure – could see no way to win
	Looked forward to competition	Wanted to quit competing and escape
	Positive confident thoughts	Negative thoughts/ self-doubt/worry
	Had a mission to stay on top of opponent	Lacking motivation and commitment to event
	Kept thinking about working hard	Questioned whether or not to try
Feelings	Confident	Apprehensive
	Excited	Tense
	Sense of anticipation	Sense of dread
	Enthusiasm	Not wanting to take part
	Relaxed	Nervous
	Ready for action	Fearful
	Energised	Lethargic/tired
	In control emotionally	Felt shameful, despondent
Focus	Task-appropriate cues	Irrelevant cues
	Focused and positive	Attention wanders ineffectively

5 *Compare your answers with the following table:*

	Positive	*Negative*
Cognitive	*Increased effort resulting from concern/importance of task*	*Self-doubts resulting in ineffective decision-making and poor concentration*
Somatic	*Physical readiness resulting in enhanced performance execution*	*Excessive muscle tension, optimal activation and therefore interfering with skill*

The appropriate activation states needed in your sport should now be clearer. The characteristics of optimal activation are similar to those you experienced when you performed effectively under stress but different from those when you could not cope with the stressor. Some of the anxiety symptoms may have caused inappropriate activation levels and contributed to sub-standard performance. Nonetheless, you may have also experienced anxiety symptoms during your effective performance and wanted them to be there. This is not uncommon and supports the view that it is the individual performer who controls the quality and quantity of thoughts and feelings he believes facilitate performance.

Inevitably there are factors which can cause stress and result in anxiety which is detrimental to performance. These are explored in the next activity.

ACTIVITY 5

1 In the first column, list the factors/situations/events you believe have caused stress for you or your performers in sport and which have had detrimental consequences as a result of anxiety:

Factors	E/I/U	Mental Symptoms (Cognitive, Thoughts)	Physical Symptoms (Somatic, Feelings)

2 In the second column, try to categorise the sources as:

- external – **E** (eg look of the opposition, weather conditions, 5–4 up serving at 30–30, team selector in audience)

- internal – **I** (eg worry about losing last service game, making a bad pass, fear of letting team down due to previous form)

- unrelated to sport – **U** (eg concern about forthcoming exams, relationship problem).

3 In the last two columns, note the debilitative symptoms experienced:

- mentally (eg difficulty in concentrating, mind full of what ifs?)

- physically (eg nausea, extreme tension, shaking).

Now turn over.

1 *You probably listed various sources of stress. These can range from very specific factors (eg your expectations, having to win, poor previous performance) to more general factors (eg others' expectations, lack of preparation for important competition, moving to another level of competition).*

2 *You may have noted that some sources of stress are personal or internal factors (eg your own personality and expectations, lack of self-confidence, fear of failure) or external factors (eg critical point in the game, presence of spectators, the behaviour of opponents). It is possible to develop strategies to help performers cope with both external and internal influences and develop appropriate strategies to cope with other sources of stress (this will be considered again in Programme Six, Page 78). It is important to recognise they may be unrelated to the sport.*

3 *Stress will probably be manifested in different ways as a result of these factors. You may have found that for some situations, you only experience physical (somatic) complaints such as nausea and stomach upsets, trembling, yawning, dryness in the mouth, tension and butterflies. Other situations, however, spark off worry (cognitive) leading to difficulties in sleeping, tactical decision-making, staying in the present and focused on task-relevant cues. While cognitive and somatic anxiety are independent and can be experienced in isolation, most performers tend to experience both types of anxiety and each commonly sparks off the other.*

1.5 Summary and Further Help

In this chapter, you have been encouraged to reflect on the significance of mental qualities (especially control) to success in sport and the potential of mental training. In the next chapter, you will be introduced to some of the mental techniques used to manage stress and activation levels in competition. This will help you become familiar with some of the guidelines and recognise the relative worth of each in handling pressure. It will outline when these techniques are commonly used and suggest how the technique progresses from application in general training to employment in actual competition. You will then be able to work through the subsequent programmes in Part Two in the order that best suits your needs and those of your performers.

If the area of mental training is fairly new to you, you may wish to read the following pack, available from Coachwise Ltd (0113 231 1310):

Sellars, C (1996) **Mental Skills: An introduction for sports coaches.** Leeds, National Coaching Foundation. ISBN 0-947850-34-1

Chapter Two: Techniques to Handle Pressure and Control Emotion

2.0 What's in It for You?

Peak performances in sport are regularly accompanied by certain characteristic feelings – of supreme confidence, total concentration, high levels of energy and awareness, being in control, and mentally and physically calm or relaxed. The closer performers are able to create this ideal performance state (IPS), the more likely they are to achieve top performances. The ability to handle the pressure and control thoughts and feelings before and during a competition is therefore crucial to success in sport. Although anxiety and stress can enhance performance by generating energy and alertness, a sense of determination and perhaps aggression; uncontrolled levels have a negative effect on performance – they disrupt concentration and decision-making, and interfere with the technical and physical execution of the sport skills.

Coaches can play a vital role in helping performers control their thoughts and feelings, and retain a positive attitude. Good coaches do this in a number of ways – for example, by the way they:

- boost the performer's confidence by building on strengths, providing positive and constructive feedback, helping to set realistic goals and empowering performers to accept responsibility for their own actions

- plan in fine detail to ensure performers are fully prepared and able to handle every aspect of the performance

- help performers develop effective coping skills that reflect their levels of mental toughness displayed in competition and training.

The way coaches develop programmes and interact with their performers is considered in many other books. This pack focuses primarily on helping performers learn a range of mental training techniques and strategies to enable them to handle pressure, manage stress and anxiety, and control their thoughts and emotions[1]. This chapter provides a rationale for selecting and implementing the programmes in Part Two, so it is important to work through it carefully.

---

1 For further help on the mental training techniques, refer to the summary section of this chapter (Page 55) or request a Coachwise Catalogue (0113 231 1310) for an up-to-date listing of new packs.

2.1 Different Approaches

It is important to emphasise that managing stress and coping with pressure involve knowing what to manage. As you will have realised from Chapter One, individuals manifest stress in different ways. Some become nervous, experience butterflies in the stomach, sweaty hands, muscle tension, nausea, as well as a need to go to the toilet frequently (symptoms of somatic anxiety). Others will be overwhelmed with worry, negative thoughts, self-criticism or struggle to maintain a task-relevant attentional focus (symptoms of cognitive anxiety). A mental training programme to cope with pressure and manage stress should therefore involve both physical (ie body-to-mind) and cognitive (ie mind-to-body) techniques. Four different approaches to stress management are considered and, for each, the relevant techniques are identified. Like any technique, to be effective the techniques must be learnt, practised, used regularly and integrated into other aspects of performance preparation and competition. It is important to remember as you read, that each mental technique will be best developed by adhering to the learning principles described in Section 1.3 (Page 9).

1 Use relaxation to reduce anxiety symptoms

One approach to stress management hinges on reducing the symptoms of anxiety associated with the stressor. If performers have the ability to control their experience of anxiety, they can then induce an optimal activation state that will facilitate the execution of technical and physical skills. It is vitally important for coaches to match the anxiety control technique with the specific type of anxiety the performer negatively experiences (this is termed the **matching hypothesis**). The mental techniques and strategies described in this pack will apply the matching hypothesis and focus on techniques aimed at relaxing the body and calming the mind to deal effectively with the physical and cognitive symptoms of stress. The sort of relaxation techniques available are summarised in the adjacent panel and are then described in greater detail in Section 2.2 (Page 28).

Managing the body = muscle-to-mind techniques
- Rhythmic breathing
- Progressive muscular relaxation
- Centring

Managing/calming the mind = mind-to-muscle techniques
- Imagery-based relaxation
- Meditative relaxation

2 Restructure thoughts so anxiety is perceived positively

Reducing the symptoms of anxiety may not be the best course of action for some performers – for example those who want the fire to burn in their bellies. It is important, therefore, for coaches to be aware of the merits of **cognitive restructuring.** This involves the performer actively reappraising the stressor in a positive manner and then viewing the symptoms of anxiety in a facilitative way. This technique is examined in more detail in Section 2.3 (Page 40).

> **Technique**
> * Cognitive re-structuring

3 Learn to take control of your attitude towards stressors (active stress management)

The main reason why performers experience anxiety is because they view the stressor as something outside their control. For example, if the stressful situation is taking an important penalty in football, the attitude of most players to the demands imposed by this stressor would be outcome-based (ie 'I need to score this goal'). This attitude gives the stressor uncontrollable properties and the resultant cognitive appraisal would be 'I don't think I can score' (ie achieve the demands imposed by the stressor). Anxiety would be provoked because the player cannot guarantee the goal. If, however, the player's attitude to the stressful situation is performance and process-based (ie 'I need to take a clean penalty and make firm contact with the ball'), the stressor becomes controllable. The resulting cognitive appraisal would be 'Yes, I'm sure I can take a clean penalty and place it well'. This in itself would be the key to scoring a goal anyway and the penalty would be taken without the negative effects of anxiety.

Coaches, therefore, can teach their performers to develop and activate performance-based attitudes to competition. Attitude management is a form of active stress management where you manage stress by having thoughts with controllable properties (ie not dependent on others) so stress is not experienced. This is the opposite of reactive stress management where anxiety is already experienced and you need to find ways of coping with it. One of the best ways of teaching attitude management is through performance and process goal-setting. However, the best way to practise it is through contingency planning where appropriate attitudes are put into practice as performers devise contingency responses to any stressful situation that arises. These are examined in Section 2.4 (Page 46).

> **Techniques**
> * Performance goal-setting
> * Contingency planning

1   For further explanation of goal-setting and different types of goals, you are recommended to the NCF pack *Mental Skills: an introduction for sports coaches,* available from Coachwise Ltd (0113 231 1310).

4   **Learn to increase activation levels if necessary**

Handling pressure is not just about reducing anxiety or restructuring to gain optimal activation levels. It is also about making sure you can handle the pressure of not being sufficiently activated. In this pack, you will be introduced to several mental and physical activation techniques – imagery-based and emotional activation strategies. These are considered in more detail in Section 2.5 (Page 51).

> **Techniques**
> - Imagery-based activation
> - Emotional activation

2.2   Relaxation Techniques

In this section, you can find out how to reduce the symptoms of anxiety by learning a range of relaxation techniques: rhythmic breathing, centring, progressive muscular relaxation (PMR), meditative relaxation and imagery-based relaxation.

Rhythmic breathing

Breathing plays an important role in dealing with pressure situations and managing stress. Some performers can manage stress just by changing their breathing pattern. When you feel under pressure, anxious or stressed – does your breathing become laboured, short and/or very shallow? Typically when you are calm or in control, your breathing is deep, smooth and rhythmic. One of the major uses of rhythmic breathing is the increased flow of oxygen to the working muscles which helps to relieve muscle tension. This is particularly useful for sports involving fine, complex motor skills (eg golf putt, pistol shooting). It is also a very effective concentration cue[1]. An important property of rhythmic breathing is that you breathe to a certain rhythm. You may try inhaling for a count of three seconds, hold for three and exhale for three. It is also useful to attend to and feel your diaphragm (the breathing muscle at the base of the rib cage) rise and fall during the sequence. As your performers are introduced to the techniques of centring, progressive muscular relaxation and meditative relaxation, they will find their breathing pattern also plays a key role in their ability to learn to use these relaxation techniques.

---

1   You may wish to follow up further on this by reading the NCF pack *Improving Concentration*, available from Coachwise Ltd (0113 231 1310).

ACTIVITY 6

1   Check your pulse (count for 15 secs and multiply by four). Place your hands on the base of your rib cage (your diaphragm), breathe in deeply (inhale) to a count of three and feel the rib cage expand, hold for a count of three and then breathe out (exhale) to the count of three. Repeat a number of times and notice the effect on your physiological and mental state. You may feel more mentally calm and focused and, if you retake your pulse, you will probably find it has lowered.

2   The effect will be even more marked if you try the same deep breathing exercise following some physical exertion (eg running up a flight of stairs or some form of exercise that induces mild fatigue) or when feeling under some mental pressure. Try the same exercise under these conditions (NB This is quite easy to do in a break in training and gets the message across to performers in their sport environment).

3   You may wish to experiment with different inhale/hold/exhale ratios – some people may prefer a longer or shorter breathing pattern to gain the relaxation effect.

4   Jot down specific situations in your sport when performers might benefit from using this type of breathing exercise:

•

•

•

Now turn over.

4   *This type of breathing exercise can be used in a number of sport situations and examples are provided to help you think of appropriate occasions in your sport:*

- *When your performers are waiting to start (eg before a race, event or match, prior to taking a throw or jump, before being substituted onto court or field).*

- *At stoppages during the event (eg between events or games, when the ball is dead, at time outs, before taking a penalty, at a foul or injury).*

- *It is particularly useful at any point at which there is a need to control anxiety and/or sharpen or narrow concentration prior to an important action.*

Few performers are taught how to breathe properly to control unwanted tension or enhance their performance. It may be as simple as choosing a word or mental cue (eg centre, focus) to reduce unwanted tension while you breathe in and out and focus your attention to cope with the pressure and stress of the situation.

Although this looks simple, your performers need to practise their chosen technique regularly. To reduce anxiety effectively and control stress before it controls them, performers must work through the learning process and practise in the same way they practise technical skills. Breathing is simple but it involves physiological and attentional properties which make it one of the most important and easy-to-employ techniques in the heat of competition. In Programme Two (Page 62), you will be shown how you can introduce this technique to your performers. They will experience how practising deep breathing utilising the diaphragm can lead to a state of emotional control. You will want to work these techniques into your practices and daily routines so they become one of the many mental strategies your performers can learn to rely on, when they feel things are getting out of control.

Centring

Centring is about gathering yourself together, ready to focus your attention on the task at hand. Although there are many different ways to centre, the technique described here requires you to change your centre of consciousness from your head to your centre of gravity – a point just below your navel. This lowering of your centre of consciousness makes you feel much more stable and balanced. It is this feeling of stability, balance and control when centred that prompts you to relax. When you do relax, you also sink a little and lower your centre of gravity (and therefore consciousness) still further, thereby creating a spiral effect on stability and control.

Centring helps your performers to attend consciously to events during their performance when faced with pressure – adversity, anxiousness or a need to turn things around. When performers are confident or relaxed before they perform, there may be no need to centre. When tension is tight, the situation is filled with high expectations or the performer has struggled in recent performances, it may be time for your performer to centre and remove unwanted tension.

One of the greatest attributes of centring is that, with practice, it provides a method of relaxing quickly and regaining control of a situation that is starting to slip away from you. A deep breath and exhalation is all that is needed to get rid of the feeling of panic which usually accompanies such situations, for example as you go onto the starting blocks of an important race, as you prepare to serve at a critical point, as you go to the free throw line when the score is tied. You can then refocus your attention on what needs to be done and how you are going to do it (ie on driving from the blocks, on the rhythm of the serve, on the smooth execution of the shot) instead of on the consequences of failure if you do not. As centring provides control and stability, it is frequently used in the martial arts where awareness of the centre of gravity and balance is crucial.

ACTIVITY 7

1   If you have never tried **centring** to focus or regain your attention, try the following exercise:

   - Stand with your feet shoulder width apart and knees slightly bent.

   - Relax your neck, arms and shoulder muscles.

   - Direct your thoughts inward to check and adjust your muscle tension and breathing. This is best done if you focus on your abdominal muscles and how they tighten and relax as you breathe. Feel the heaviness in your muscles.

   - Take a deep, slow breath using the diaphragm (ie a point just behind your navel) with minimal movement of the chest.

   - As you continue to focus consciously on your breathing and the heaviness of your muscles, clear your mind of all irrelevant thoughts and cues.

   - Next, focus your thoughts on an upcoming competitive situation and what you need to do to perform effectively.

2   Jot down situations when you feel centring might be useful in your sport:

Now turn over.

Once learnt, centring is quick and easy to use in a number of situations, particularly at critical moments during a competition – typically prior to executing a closed skill (such as taking a penalty, before a high jump attempt, before serving or bowling).

Although centring may appear to be simple, the challenge comes from knowing when to centre and what to attend to after centring. The key is to develop an awareness of what breathing (regular or irregular) indicates an inappropriate tension level. After practice in various situations, a performer should be able to centre and change levels of tension with a single breath – even in the most stressful situations. To be effective, you need to practise this technique in various situations. In Programme Two (Page 62), you will have a chance to teach centring to your performers[1].

Progressive muscular relaxation (PMR)

Performers often complain of muscle tension and nervousness prior to and during competition. While some performers have learnt to control these physiological symptoms through trial and error, many individuals have no idea how to combat tension and cope with nerves. PMR is recognised as one of the basic tools of most mental training programmes. Many performers are introduced to it to help them:

- induce sleep before a big event
- reduce somatic anxiety levels before a competition
- control somatic anxiety during competition.

PMR training helps you gain control over the levels of tension in every muscle group of your body. The technique works by alternatively tensing and then relaxing each muscle group in your body, while focusing on the sensations felt and contrasting the difference (eg active progressive relaxation). In this way, you condition the ability to relax a tense muscle on demand. Muscle tension under involuntary control becomes muscle relaxation under voluntary control. If you have not experienced PMR, you should try the next activity.

---

1   Most of the references on centring do not focus on a step-by-step list, rather more of a description of how to centre.

ACTIVITY 8

1   First read the following instructions and then choose a quiet place to work through them practically[1]. Alternatively, you can use a reputable relaxation tape of PMR rather than the following text.

2   Instructions:

- Lie down and relax your entire body. If you hear noises, don't try to block them out but focus on your breathing – inhaling, then exhaling slowly. If you want to move slightly, that's OK. Close your eyes, take it easy and relax.

- Tense the muscles of your right lower leg and foot by pointing your toe. Hold the tension for five to six seconds and then relax. You should be able to feel the tension in the foot and the calf and then totally relax. When you relax, feel the warmth in the muscles. Repeat this procedure again on the right leg and then repeat it twice for the left leg.

- After tensing and relaxing the lower leg and foot, tense (for five seconds) and relax the thigh and buttocks region (twice for each leg). Tense the buttocks and thighs by pushing down with your buttocks.

- Tense and relax the forearm and hand by making a fist. Do this twice for each arm. Tense and relax the bicep of each arm by bending at the elbow and pretending you are doing a chin up. Repeat twice for each arm.

- Tense (for five seconds) and relax the back muscles by arching the back up. Tense and relax the back twice. Tense the stomach and chest muscles by breathing in and releasing – relaxing. Do this twice.

- Tense the neck and shoulders by shrugging your shoulders (pulling them together) and then releasing them and relaxing. Tense the face and forehead by gritting your teeth and pulling your eyebrows together, then relax. Do this twice.

- Mentally scan your body for any tension and release it. Focus on the relaxed feelings in your muscles and the calming thoughts of your mind set.

- When you wish to return to a higher level of consciousness, count upwards from one to seven, counting one number on each exhalation, gradually experiencing greater alertness and awareness of the external environment. When you reach seven, you should feel fully awake, relaxed and refreshed.

3   After you have worked through this exercise, slowly flex, stretch, inhale and open your eyes before you sit up. Take time to evaluate how well you were able to relax during this exercise.

---

1   These instructions are adapted from Ken Hodge (1994). *Sport motivation on: Training your mind for peak performance* (p 123) Auckland, NZ, Reed Books.

*Whether you found this exercise difficult, you felt as if nothing happened, or you forgot the sequence of muscle groups to tense and relax, learn to be patient. Relaxation tends to occur only when the body is ready. The more you practise, the more easily you will relax. The exercise may also have made you feel fairly tired or fatigued as opposed to refreshed. This is one of the reasons why a 15–20 minute form of relaxation (deep relaxation) is not normally recommended just before competing. This deep form of relaxation should be for learning purposes and perhaps for use in the week prior to an event or to encourage sleep the night before. Performers can gradually reduce the time it takes to relax from 15 minutes to 5 minutes to 30 seconds. In this way, they can develop a range of differing relaxation skills – **deep** relaxation when required, five minute **control** relaxation shortly prior to competing, and a 30 second **composure** relaxation skill for moments during performance (refer to Table 2 on the opposite page).*

With practice, your performers will learn what each muscle feels like when it is relaxed and when it is tense. They will then be able to relax the muscle group instantly, simply by observing the tension in it. Having developed an awareness of the feeling of muscular tension, performers are better able to recognise the signs of unwanted tension which can then trigger the relaxation response. In this way, PMR helps performers develop a heightened awareness about how their bodies respond to tension. As they practise PMR, they begin to recognise signs of tension or nervousness and learn to control it before it hinders performance. Relaxation training can, however, do more for your performers if they learn to practise it in different situations and relax muscle groups separately, as well as all together. It is important for you to identify the key muscle groups utilised in your sport and the typical situations where control or composure PMR techniques would be most applicable. Another useful tip is to employ differential relaxation (Hardy et al, 1996) where performers practise experiencing and releasing along a different range of tensions. For example, they might tense to 75%, release to 25% and then increase tension to 50%. By doing this, they can place themselves on the fast track to heightened awareness.

NB You need to be aware that some of the same emotional symptoms exist for negative somatic anxiety as for positive physiological arousal (eg elevated heart rate). The difference between the two states is essentially different perceptions of the same symptoms. Consequently, while PMR is useful for muscle relaxation, it can also reduce other physiological symptoms. Before employing this technique, you need to work out with performers which symptoms of arousal they may require. *Remember, don't put out the fire if the athlete likes it to burn brightly.*

In Part Two, you will run through several exercises which allow your performers to move from deep PMR away from sport to sessions or situations which involve instant relaxation during the performance.

 You may choose to develop an audiotape of the instructions to give to your performers to help them practise at home (see Programme Three).

Meditative relaxation

If cognitive anxiety is a major problem for your performers, this is usually manifested by negative thoughts, self-doubts and an attentional focus on completely task-irrelevant cues. The coach needs to employ a technique which allows the performer's mind to be filled at any point in time by positive, task-relevant or at least neutral thoughts. In sport, the most important moments to possess this ability are clearly the potentially stressful situations. A meditative relaxation technique is essentially a deep concentration exercise which allows performers to develop the ability to focus the mind and its available attentional resources on a task-relevant or neutral cue word (referred to as a **mantra**). In this way, it attempts to buffer the mind against any negative thoughts entering the available attentional space, while a strictly cognitive technique, meditative relaxation has been found to reduce certain physiological symptoms (eg respiration, heart rate, blood pressure, blood lactate, cortisol) so adding to its versatility. Meditative relaxation usually begins with a 15–20 minute session which offers performers an experience of a deep state of relaxation. However, by following a progressive programme, performers can condition their minds to relax and focus positively in a matter of minutes and seconds. The performer's armoury of mental relaxation techniques can, therefore, reflect the physical relaxation skill profile he or she possesses.

Type	Duration	Examples of Use
Deep	15–20 mins	Used for general skill development and perhaps the day or night before a big event
Control	5 mins	Used to focus the mind prior to competing
Composure	30 secs	Used to regroup or refocus task-relevant attention during competition.

**Table 2: Examples of when to use different types of relaxation
(adapted from work by Ost, 1988 and Jones, 1993)**

Four steps to a successful meditative relaxation session:

- Ensure there is a quiet environment.

- Encourage each performer to assume a comfortable position.

- Help performers identify and repeat their own key word or phrase (mantra) to cue in their relaxation response – examples of popular phrases include *relax, focus* or *calm.* While repeating the word or phrase, performers should exhale to relax completely.

- Ensure every performer adopts a passive, open-minded attitude. It may help to think of a passive attitude like *letting it happen* as opposed to *making it happen* or *trying too hard.*

NB It is worth noting that because the technique is designed to induce an altered state of consciousness, some performers may experience unpleasant thoughts or images during the activity. This is very rare but if it occurs, they must discontinue the session.

ACTIVITY 9

1   First read the following instructions and then choose a quiet place and a comfortable position to work through them practically. Select some relaxing or calming music – baroque music (such as Bach's Air on a G String) is particularly suitable as it coincides perfectly with the average resting heart rate. Play this music quietly as you work through the exercise. Select your mantra (key word such as *calm, relax, focus, one*).

2   Instructions:

- Switch on the music, lie down and relax your entire body.

- If you hear noises, don't try to block them out but focus on your breathing – inhaling, then exhaling slowly.

- As you breathe out, repeat the mantra to yourself.

- Continue for about five minutes or until you feel you can block out all internal and external distractions.

- If you lose it, focus your attention back on your mantra.

- If you wish to gain a deeper level of relaxation, try counting down from ten to one with successive exhalations (ie count ten on the first breath, nine on the second). When you reach one, start the process again from ten.

- When you wish to return to a higher level of consciousness, count upwards from one to seven – again counting on each exhalation. When you reach seven, you should feel fully awake, relaxed and refreshed. Slowly flex, stretch, inhale and open your eyes before you sit up.

3   Take time to evaluate how well you were able to relax during this exercise.

4   If you found this a useful form of relaxation, you may wish to construct your own tape using your chosen music and a set of scripted instructions written specifically for you (or your performers – see Programme Four, Page 68). You might choose to use someone else's voice. You can vary the length of the taped relaxation session according to the situation, your own (or your performer's) needs and the level of relaxation you require.

You should now feel very relaxed but like PMR, it is not recommended to use this particular session prior to a competition unless your performers experience excessive amounts of worry.

This session is the starting point to the conditioning process and the following progressions[1] may then take place:

Tape 15 mins	Practise three times a week for a number of weeks
Reduce time to 10 minutes	Practise in normal and adverse situations
Reduce time to 30 seconds	Practise in everyday situations, in training and minor competition Implement in competition and as part of general training and the preparation programme

In Programme Three (Page 65), you will be taught how to take your performers through these progressions so they can produce a clear, calm and focused state of mind instinctively – even in the heat of competition.

Imagery-based relaxation
Imagery-based relaxation is another mental relaxation technique with the properties of focusing the mind on relevant/neutral cues and detaching it from negative thoughts. It can be a very powerful mind-to-body technique, providing you (or your performers) are able to form clear, controlled images that involve all the senses – sight, sound, touch, feeling, taste, smell. Some performers will find this very easy to do, others will initially struggle to make their images do what they want them to do, while a few may be unable to form any images whatsoever. An imagery-based relaxation technique is also an excellent starting point for other mental training including imagery-based activation which will be covered shortly.

Precisely how imagery-based relaxation works varies from technique to technique. However, all the techniques contain an element of dissociation from unpleasant stimuli (eg pressure situations, anxiety) and some sort of self-suggestion in the form of calming pictures. If you are unfamiliar with the technique of imagery[2], try the next activity.

---

1   Adapted from Graham Jones, 1993.

2   For further help, you might wish to read the NCF training pack for coaches and performers *Imagery Training: a guide for sports coaches and performers,* available from Coachwise Ltd (0113 231 1310).

ACTIVITY 10

1   First read the following instructions and then choose a quiet place and comfortable position to work through them practically.

2   Instructions:

- Lie down and relax your entire body. If you hear noises, don't try to block them out but focus on your breathing – inhaling, then exhaling slowly.

- Once you have established an effective breathing pattern, focus your attention on an image or situation you find particularly tranquil – perhaps a gentle waterfall, rolling hills, a beautiful sunset, a sunny beach. Try to create a vivid image – see the shapes, colours, textures, people – all in as much detail as possible.

- Note any sounds – perhaps of water, birds, voices. Notice any smells – of the sea air, sun cream, flowers. Try to feel any sensations – the breeze on your face, the wind in your hair, the sand between your toes, the water on your feet. Are there any tastes – the sea air, ice cream, a cool drink?

- Don't worry if you find yourself wandering from one image to another – it is useful to experiment to find the ideal image that elicits the most relaxed response. Continue this exercise until you are able easily to hold the images effortlessly.

- When you wish to return to a higher level of consciousness, count upwards from one to seven, counting on each exhalation, gradually experiencing greater alertness and awareness of the external environment. When you reach seven, you should feel fully awake, relaxed and refreshed. Slowly flex, stretch, inhale and open your eyes before you sit up.

3   Take time to evaluate how well you were able to relax during this exercise.

4   If you found this a useful form of relaxation, you may wish to construct your own tape using your chosen music and a set of scripted instructions written specifically for you (or your performers – see Programme Four, Page 68). The script needs to contain images that are significant to the user. You might choose to use someone else's voice. You can vary the length of the taped relaxation session according to the situation, your own (or your performer's) needs and the level of relaxation you require.

The key to imagery-based relaxation – indeed any imagery technique – is the ability of the users to employ their senses. You should therefore be teaching your performers to use their visual, auditory, tactile and olfactory senses to shift emotion. Start with calming pictures in a place that elicits relaxation before bringing in other senses. Performers need to re-create their special place, where they feel totally safe, in control and without pressure or stress. This requires attention to detail with the senses working overtime to re-create a vivid reality. This relaxation technique is successful because it teaches the individual to direct attention away from negative and irrelevant thoughts and encourages attention to be placed on neutral or positive images.

With practice, performers can summon an image of this place in a matter of seconds and the resulting relaxation response can be physiologically relaxing as well as mind filling. It is worth pointing out, however, that imagery-based relaxation does not need to consist of non-sport-specific, tranquil material. If the role of imagery is simply to focus the mind's attention on something positive and relevant as opposed to negative and irrelevant, performers may simply recall the image of their best performance in sport, rehearse the successful execution of a skill or reflect on what they feel or how they behave when they are confident. These are all methods of using attentional resources in a constructive manner. In Programme 4 (Page 68), you will be shown how you can incorporate imagery-based relaxation into your coaching practice.

2.3 Cognitive Restructuring Techniques

The statement *thoughts govern action* carries plenty of weight when it comes to mental training. The way people think governs the emotions they experience, the actions taken and behaviour displayed. It is no wonder psychologists, who are experts in stress management, do not always advocate the need to reduce the symptoms by relaxation. If thoughts about the symptoms of anxiety can be changed and also the cognitive appraisal of the stressor, an alternative way to manage stress becomes available.

The key to this route is basically the ability of your performers to keep their glass psychologically full at all times. The more performers are prone to negative thoughts about performance and the situations in which they find themselves, the more the cognitive appraisal of a stressful situation is likely to be negative. In addition, the resultant experience and rush of cognitive and somatic anxiety symptoms is likely to be viewed negatively. Do not forget the saying *what you think is what you are*. If you think you will perform badly, you probably will. There is an unfortunate but very real self-fulfilling prophecy that is operated by negative thinking performers. On the bright side, the prophecy can work equally positively for performers who do keep their glass psychologically full as opposed to almost empty.

The key to cognitive restructuring begins with an awareness of the quality of your self-talk. Most people indulge from time to time in some form of self-talk – a term used to describe what people say to themselves either out loud or as a small voice inside their head. This self-talk tends to be either positive or negative (rarely neutral). In pressure situations, negative self-talk tends to reduce confidence and increase feelings of anxiety. It is, therefore, as important to counter negative self-talk as it is to induce positive self-talk.

Imagine the situation of a tennis player who is match point up – the following would be an example of negative, anxiety provoking , task-irrelevant self-talk contrasted with positive, emotive, task-relevant self-talk:

Positive	Negative
'Stay focused and work hard,	*'I've got to win this point,*
serve to the backhand and move	*if I don't win from here, I know*
in on the first short ball'	*I won't get selected for the squad'*

Self-talk is a powerful way through which performers can reinforce positive feelings, images and thoughts while lessening the effects of negative distractions. It is a key skill in controlling anxiety, as well as boosting self-confidence. In each case, self-talk is more than just thinking or saying positive statements. It involves developing a self-awareness of what type of self-talk is detrimental (or beneficial) to performance and when your performers engage in self-defeating or self-enhancing statements. The first stage is, therefore, developing awareness. This can be achieved by an exercise called **exposing the negatives.** Try it for yourself.

ACTIVITY 11

In any pressured situation in your sport or work, note the typical negative statements you make and the thoughts that come into your mind. Try to be as specific as possible – note the exact context and the effect it has on your performance. It may help first to read the example from tennis:

Situation	Statement	Consequences
5-2 up in the final set against a higher ranking player, about to serve	*'Only four points away from beating the number one seed – I can't lose from here?'*	*Muscle tension in elbow, erratic ball toss, double fault*

You will invariably have recognised certain situations during a competition when self-doubts creep in and negative statements run through your head, for example at game point down in tennis – 'don't let me serve a double fault now'; as you approach the bell in a 1500m race – 'I don't think I have enough left to make the break'. The negative words and images influence the selection and execution of the action – they seem to preset the system to produce the behaviour that matches the image and thought (ie the double fault, the lack of pace in the last lap). The words may also seem to increase the feelings of somatic anxiety.

Sometimes, you are not even aware (consciously) you are setting yourself up for failure. Your focus switches from thinking about the demands of the sport, the task in hand and key strategies and skills, to the consequences of the outcome and external factors which have nothing to do with the here and now of performing to the best of your ability.

Having exposed the negatives, you can now attack them with positive counter-responses. Devising a mental library of counter-responses is probably the most important stage of a longer-term cognitive restructuring programme. Negative thoughts will not go away until the replacement mechanism is in place and available for use. With the list of negatives you exposed, try the next activity which involves countering the negative phrase with a positive statement.

ACTIVITY 12

Rewrite each of your negative statements from the last activity into positive ones. An example is provided to help you:

Negative/Irrelevant Statement	Positive/Counter-response
'Only four points away from beating the number one seed – I can't lose from here'	*'Let's enter the fire – kick it into her backhand and work hard for the volley'*

You have now started the process of cognitive restructuring. The final stage obviously involves practising (verbally) the use of positive statements in training and competition. To have the most beneficial effects, positive self-talk should be used by your performers in their daily routines and major competitions. They should practise incorporating this cognitive strategy prior to critical moments in training (eg before a big point, after a mistake, as part of a pre-shot routine) and in simulated stressful situations (eg at a penalty shoot out, staged at the end of training, with a monetary reward for those who score). Initially, specific techniques or drills can be isolated so performers can develop their self-talk in specific situations. A good example of this is to ask performers verbally to shout out their thoughts during a drill or talk their thoughts out loud during any breaks in performance (eg between points, after a goal, prior to a penalty).

There are some finer points you should consider. Remember, handling pressure is not just a reactive process. Cognitive restructuring is reactive because you are challenging the negative thoughts you already have or tend to have in stressful situations. If you want to be active about handling pressure, a beneficial exercise is to make sure your performers build up a library of positive statements they can use whether or not they suffer from negative self-talk. You are not, therefore, countering or reacting to negatives, you are merely employing positives you have naturally listed, learned and practised in training.

For example, a hockey player may list the statement 'calm and slow into the ball ... fast out' as a focused directive phrase to use prior to taking a penalty flick. She could repeat and condition this positive cueing phrase during repetitive practice of penalty flicks in a penalty flick competition with team-mates.

Secondly, it is worth mentioning that if you do become aware of a negative thought, you should actually engage in **thought stopping** as the first stage of cognitive restructuring. Try to use the words *stop, hold it* or *counter* to neutralise the negative. Then use the counter-responses you have stored in your library. The training process and implementation processes can be shown as follows:

Training process:
Awareness/expose ➤ Create/list counter-responses ➤ Verbal practice in training

Implementation process:
Thought stopping ➤ Neutralise the negative ➤ Counter with the positive

---

You may also have noticed that cognitive restructuring can be used above and beyond simply changing interpretations of anxiety symptoms or thoughts about a stressful situation (cognitive appraisal). It may be useful to encourage performers to go through these latter exercises before giving them the chance to practise restructuring their perceptions of anxiety (see Programme Five, Page 75).

1 To encourage performers to interpret anxiety in a positive way, the coach may help performers recognise symptoms of anxiety as positive signs of physical and mental readiness. As such, the anxiety should be viewed positively rather than as unpleasant symptoms that threaten performance. For example, performers might restructure their thoughts like this:

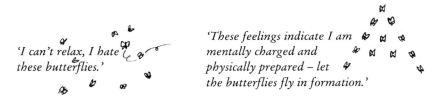

'I can't relax, I hate these butterflies.'

'These feelings indicate I am mentally charged and physically prepared – let the butterflies fly in formation.'

2 In addition to restructuring perceptions of anxiety, it is also possible to reappraise the original stressor – this is known as **re-framing.** In other words, the performer consciously tries to reappraise the stressful situation by turning it on its head and viewing it in a different way. For example, a football team goes two goals down in less than ten minutes of play, and feeling dejected, despairing and confused after the second goal, they fail to regain focus and concede a third in the next minute. They needed to regroup after the first goal and find some way of re-framing the stressful situation they were experiencing to mobilise resources for the task at hand. A way of re-framing the situation might have been to say 'I'd rather be two goals down after ten minutes, than two goals down with ten minutes to go.'

Coaches should be able to devise a session with their performers outside training that involves practising re-framing skills for the typical stressful situations that could arise in their sport. The coach could provide the situations and the negative appraisal of them – the performers could provide examples of what their re-framed responses might be. You can try this in Programme Five (Page 75).

2.4 Attitude Management

Attitude management is about teaching the mind to view the demands imposed by the stressful situation in a controllable as opposed to an uncontrollable way. If performers focus on the outcome in a stressful situation, they are probably going to experience anxiety. If, however, they are able to focus on how the stressor challenges them to perform to the best of their abilities, the stressor becomes more controllable and anxiety is less likely to be elicited.

If you accept that *thoughts govern action and emotion,* surely *attitude governs thought.* If this is true, the attitude of the performer is critical to everything. Try the following self-awareness activity.

ACTIVITY 13

1 Give examples of what achievement means to you in your sport (eg winning):

2 Explain how you achieve this specific goal by identifying the general contributory components (eg through high levels of fitness) in the first column:

Components	Factors	Controllable	Fundamental

3 Categorise these into factors (eg technical, physical) in the second column.

4 Mark the components/skills that can be controlled in the third column using a ✓ or ✗.

5 Assess whether these controllable components/skills are fundamental to the outcome in the fourth column using a ✓ or ✗.

6 Identify, therefore, what you should be focusing on in competition which is fundamental to the outcome:

Now turn over.

Compare your answers with the following which seem to be quite typical:

1 *Examples of achievement include winning, beating the opposition, gaining a medal, improving ranking, scoring a goal.*

2 *Examples of components/skills include pre-event preparation, own personal performance, opponent's performance, fitness levels, motivation and effort level.*

3 *Factors include physical, technical, psychological, tactical.*

4 *Controllable components/skills include your own:*

- *quality of passing*
- *pace/acceleration*
- *decision-making*
- *concentration*
- *ability to stay positive*
- *physical and mental effort*
- *emotional control.*

5/6 *Anything that is personally controllable is critical to the outcome and should therefore be the focus of attention. This is clearly preferable to uncontrollable factors being the focus of attention.*

This exercise should be used by coaches to help performers realise how readily they can use what they can control, for example aspects of personal performance such as refocusing prior to an important set piece to help them achieve a goal that may not be totally under their control (eg scoring the goal). The implication, therefore, is to focus on the controllables rather than the uncontrollables – you will have a chance to do this with your performers in Programme Six (Page 78). If the performers learn to change attitudes to focus on controllable factors – in life as well as in sport – this attitude will positively influence the quality of their thoughts in a specific pressure situation. In other words, general attitude influences competition attitude which in turn influences how the performer handles the pressure situation.

General attitude ➤ Competition attitude ➤ How the performer handles the pressure situation

---

Coaches need to help performers switch their attitude to one focused on controllable performance factors rather than uncontrollable outcome factors.

	Thought Focused on Uncontrollable Outcome Factors	Thought Focused on Controllable Performance Factors
Attitude to sport	'I'll only be successful if I win'	'I'll only be successful if I train hard and keep improving my times'
Attitude to competition	'Winning this race is the only goal'	'I'll give 100% effort to swim to the best of my current ability'
Attitude to specific pressure situation	'If I lose – I'll not be selected'	'Feel smooth through the water and look for a good turn'

Having introduced this perspective to performers, a valuable next step to take is very similar to the re-framing exercise described previously. Performers need to practise their performance and process-oriented attitudes to different stressful situations that arise in their sport. If this experience cannot readily be gained in the actual situation, you can help them determine what their attitudinal thoughts and focus should be in a variety of situations and then practise them in simulated stressful situations in training.

The first stage, therefore, involves **contingency planning** where performers are presented, perhaps in a group setting, with a range of *what if?* scenarios which can provoke stress by preventing them from achieving an uncontrollable goal.

For example:

- What if the bus breaks down and we arrive too late for a full warm-up?
- What if I fall off the first piece of apparatus?
- What if the first lap is run at too fast a pace?
- What if the ground is really heavy?
- What if the crowd is against me?

The key to attitude management is to work calmly through these in advance, devising controllable performance and process-based strategies to increase the controllability of the stressor. Try the next activity.

ACTIVITY 14

1   In the first column, list some of the *what ifs?* in your sport that might cause anxiety – one example is provided to help you:

What if?	Contingency/Attitude	Strategy
The score is level in a penalty shoot out and you have to take the next shot – the match rests on you	*'I only face one challenge – to perform to the best of my mental and physical ability'*	*Stay focused on the present – keep it smooth and simple*

2   In the centre column, note down the desired attitude or contingency.

3   In the right-hand column, suggest a strategy to help the performer cope with each situation should it occur.

In Part Two, you will be guided on how you might help performers develop and manage appropriate attitudes to stressful situations via contingency planning and simulation training (Programme Six, Page 78).

2.5 Mental and Physical Activation Techniques

The performer's mental and physical activation state determines the quality of his performance. The techniques described so far have all attempted to create the optimal activation state by reducing or restructuring the symptoms of anxiety. However, achieving the optimal state is not always a case of reducing or restructuring what are essentially different symptoms and perceptions of mental and physical arousal. It can also be about increasing the amount of activation by stimulating arousal from external sources. There is a need not just to learn to *put the fire out* but also to be able to *fan the flame.*

Increasing mental and physical activation involves utilising the body's physiology and the mind's senses. Physical activation mainly reflects the symptoms of physiological arousal – increased heart rate, respiration, muscle tension and sweating. Techniques to increase physical activation therefore include:

- actual physical work – a thorough warm-up and stretching, short burst activity (jogging on the spot, shuttle runs)
- manipulated breathing – short, shallow breaths which activate physical symptoms in response to increased oxygen debt (see Programme Seven, Page 81).

In addition, imagery, self-talk and music strategies can have the effect of increasing (as well as reducing) both mental and physical/emotional activation levels:

- **Imagery-based activation** involves the recreation of images which are meaningful to the performer in causing increased arousal. For example, imaging the crowd lining the streets as you run towards the finish line and begin picking up speed, or replaying the whole of a 400m relay race where you ran the last leg and the crowd was going wild. It is essentially down to your creativity and ability to utilise all the senses in developing an image which serves to energise your mental and physical state[1]. This can be facilitated even more by self-talk.

- **Self-talk** can be task-related and instructional but more often than not, it is emotive and seeks to shift your concentration and emotional state. Can you imagine the type of emotive self-talk you would use during the image of the relay race (eg *move it, push it out*) and what the supporting crowd would be saying to you? This can be facilitated even more by music. There are three types of self-talk that might be helpful:

  - Importance talk – 'this is it, this is what you've worked for, get into the rhythm'.

  - Personal talk – 'never, ever give less than 110% in any situation in this competition'.

  - Confrontational talk – 'be ready to be blasted off this court'.

- **Music** has a powerful effect on the body's physiology because you begin to associate certain musical tunes/melodies with signatures in the brain that have previously led to increased physiological activation. Think about your favourite pump up and hard driving music or play them as you image yourself in the last leg of the relay. You will start to buzz.

The ultimate situation to experience optimal physical and mental activation would be to use a Walkman while running. In this situation, physical activation level is going to be high due to the activity. Add to this the impact of your favourite music while imaging a crowd lining the street and cheering you on. This might create a perfect state – one associated with a faster time and less conscious pain.

---

[1] For further help on imagery, you are recommended to the NCF pack *Imagery Training: a guide for sports coaches and performers,* available from Coachwise Ltd (0113 231 1310).

You will need to be innovative about ways to integrate this type of work into actual coaching and training sessions for it will depend very much on your sport. The important goal is to help performers find their own way to activate their optimal mental and physical states, rather than reacting to the emotions caused by stressors. For example, you might encourage performers to try one or more of the following:

- **To act as if:** Ask performers to role play and personify different emotions while performing (ie you may call out *sad* or *energised* and performers must play – or run, swim – as if they are feeling that emotion).

- **To use confrontational talk:** During performance, individuals may confront others, or the team as a whole may confront another team (in training).

- **To use individual-to-team statements:** Individuals take turns to make either an important, personal or confrontational statement to the rest of the team/ squad. The unit therefore becomes mentally and physically activated. The coach can employ this with teams in training prior to a simulated (or actual) competition with a purposeful interruption.

- **To make dead time live:** Performers use any break in performance to get themselves emotionally charged by using exaggerated breathing, physical exertion, imagery or self-talk.

- **To use music via a Walkman in training and pre-competition:** Although not easy to do (and dependent on the activity, sometimes less effective), a musical environment – via a sound system or personal stereo – can have positive emotional effects on actual training. However, music has a more ostensible role in the dressing rooms or during the pre-competition period. Coaches should therefore be encouraged to simulate the pre-competition period during training so performers have emotionally prepared, even for a practice competition.

- **To make confidence videos:** By combining the elements of emotional, meaningful music with some of the individual or team's best performance accomplishments, you can provide the recipe for a highly confident state of mind and emotionally charged physiology. They are not easy to devise but can push emotion in the right direction prior to training or a competition.

You will have an opportunity to try these with your performers in Programme Seven (Page 81).

2.6   Assessing your Performer

In the preceding sections, you will have recognised the importance of helping performers attain, maintain and if necessary regain their ideal performance state (IPS) to achieve top performance. You have been introduced to a range of techniques to help you do this and in Part Two, you will be offered a number of programmes to use with your performers.

First however, you need to consider how you will assess the unique needs of your performers in order to plan an appropriate programme for them. How will you know their IPS, whether their activation state is too low or too high, how well they handle pressure? How will you select strategies to help them?

One technique that might be helpful is that of **performance profiling**[1]. This versatile tool can help coaches and performers identify the important components of performance – in this context perhaps the characteristics that describe each individual's IPS. The process involves each performer generating the qualities she perceives to be important to successful performance, for example all the feelings, positive thoughts and images associated with optimal performance. These will be unique to the individual and coaches should refrain from trying to lead the performer or impose their own ideas or terms. The ten (or twenty) most important components are then placed on the perimeter of the ring as shown in the example of the profile of a female squash player in Figure 2.

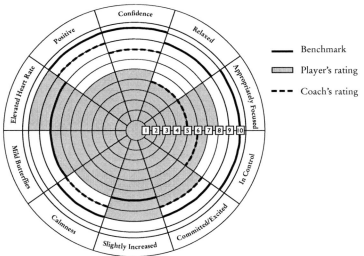

Figure 2: Profile of a female squash player

---

1   Performance profiling is a technique developed by Richard Butler. For further guidance, you are recommended to the NCF pack and audiotape *Performance Profiling* available from Coachwise Ltd (0113 231 1310).

The player is then invited to assess the relative importance of each quality – ten being deemed to be very important (shown by the solid line in the chart). In this example, the player believes to achieve her IPS, she needs a ten on *confidence, positive, being in control* and *appropriately focused*, a nine on *relaxed, excited* and *calmness* and an eight on *increased heart rate, butterflies* and *sweating*.

The player then rates her current or typical score for each against the ideal benchmark score and this is shown by the shaded areas. Similarly the coach may rate his perceptions of the player against each component (shown by the dotted line) – on this particular profile, one or two of the physiological components are left blank (eg elevated heart rate), for the coach feels he cannot assess them. In this way the profile illustrates the discrepancy between the ideal benchmark scores for each component and the player's current score and some discrepancies between the coach's perception and that of the player. Notice the largest discrepancies between the benchmark score and player's score, for example for *positive, confidence, relaxed* and *being in control*. Notice also that the coach and player's perceptions are also at odds over a number of components – notably *appropriately focused* as well as *positive* and *confidence*.

This information can then be used to clarify and agree priorities, determine a strategy and set goals. During the implementation of the strategy, the profiling exercise can be repeated to monitor progress against the goals and, as necessary, adapt the programme. In Programme One (Page 58), you are invited to carry out this exercise with your performer.

2.7 Summary and Further Help

In this chapter, you were introduced to several techniques and provided with a rationale about how these will help you and your performers handle pressure, manage the stress associated with competitive situations and learn to be able to increase activation levels when necessary. Some performers may have learnt over the years that not all stressors are bad and have developed management strategies through trial and error to approach situations in a more controlled manner. Many performers, however, crack under the pressure – perhaps they perceive everything associated with their performance as threatening or out of their control, or they feel they have to live up to others' expectations or believe their self-worth is solely dependent on how they perform. For these individuals, anxiety and stress will control their performance to such an extent they will often fold under the pressure. It is up to you to help these performers strengthen their mental qualities by selecting and practising the most effective mental techniques to handle pressure, manage stress and gain and maintain their ideal performance state.

In Part Two, seven programmes are included to help you with your mental training programme. Each programme contains one or more exercises to develop further the techniques introduced in this chapter. Remember however, that just like physical skills, these techniques must be practised and developed before they are employed in competitive situations.

The following books are recommended for further reading:

Bull, SJ (1991) **Sport psychology: a self-help guide.** Marlborough, Crowood Press. ISBN 1-85223-568-3

Bull, S, Albinson, J and Shambrook, C (1996) **The mental game plan: getting psyched for sport.** Sports Dynamics. ISBN 0-9519543-2-6

*Butler, R (1996) **Performance profiling** (audiotape and book) Leeds, National Coaching Foundation. ISBN 0-947850-36-8

*Hale, B (1998) **Imagery training: a guide for sports coaches and performers.** Leeds, National Coaching Foundation. ISBN 0-902523-10-5

Hardy, L, Jones, G and Gould, D (1996) **Understanding psychological preparation for sport: theory and practice.** Chichester, Wiley. ISBN 0-471-95787-9

Jones, G (1997) **The role of performance profiling in cognitive behavioural interventions in sport.** In *The Sport Psychologist* 7, 160–172

*Maynard, I (1998) **Improving concentration.** Leeds, National Coaching Foundation. ISBN 1-902523-01-6

*Morris, T (1997) **Psychological skills training in sport.** Leeds, National Coaching Foundation. ISBN 0-947850-78-3

Ost, LG (1988) **Applied relaxation: descriptors of an effective coping technique.** In *Scandinavian Journal of Behavioural Therapy* 17, 83–96

*Sellars, C (1996) **Mental skills: An introduction for sports coaches.** Leeds, National Coaching Foundation. ISBN 0-947850-34-1

*Sellars, C (1997) **Building self-confidence.** Leeds, National Coaching Foundation. ISBN 0-947850-11-2

Weinberg, R (1988) **The mental advantage: developing your psychological skills in tennis.** Champaign, IL, Leisure Press. ISBN 0-88011-293-X

* Available from Coachwise Ltd (0113 231 1310).

PART TWO

Programmes to Handle Pressure and Control Emotion

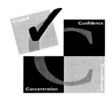

Introduction

There are seven mental training programmes in this part. It is important to complete Programme One on profiling and performer assessment before embarking on any other programme offered in this pack. You should then be able to:

- identify the characteristics of your performer's optimal mental and physical activation states

- select which programmes might be most suitable and appropriate for your performer.

From an educational viewpoint, every performer should be familiar with all techniques. You may, therefore, wish to offer guidance on all the techniques and allow performers to decide which they want to use. These can then be developed individually. However, remember to use the findings of the performer's handling pressure profile (Programme One) to determine the programmes which would be of most benefit. You may find that after using a given technique, you or your performer would gain from one or more of the others. If so, use the programmes as you feel appropriate.

Whichever method you use, the programmes will progress through similar stages:

- The coach introducing, educating and allowing performers to experience the basic technique/exercise at a general level.

- The performer practising the technique and developing it in its basic form over a number of weeks.

- The coach and performer beginning the fine tuning process by introducing the technique into the training environment and reducing the time taken to achieve an optimal state of activation.

- Practising the skill in mock competitions or simulated stressful situations devised by the coach.

- Implementing the skill and monitoring its effectiveness in progressively more important competitions.

Programme One: Profiling and Assessing your Performer

AIM

The aim of this programme is to assess your performer's ability to handle pressure by creating an ideal performance state.

Every performer is unique. It is important, therefore, to start by identifying:

• her ideal mental and physical activation states (IPS) in training and competition

• stressful situations in your sport and reflect on whether the performer is able to activate her IPS in these potentially stressful sport situations.

The process of developing a profile of the performer's ability to handle pressure (ie create an optimal state on demand whatever the situation) provides you and your performers with information on which to target areas for improvement. This information directly aids the selection of techniques designed to trigger the perceived ideal performance state.

By the end of this programme, you and your performers should be able to identify:

• the features/characteristic of their own IPS

• situations in which they have difficulty achieving their IPS.

With this information, you and your performer can focus on a programme to achieve the IPS in identified situations. Before starting Phase 1, it may help to refer back to Activity 4 (Page 17) where you identified the typical mental and physiological/emotional characteristics that seem to be crucial to optimal performance.

You will need to work with your performers outside the coaching session. You will probably want to carry out the first three steps in Session A (approximately one hour) and then encourage your performers to reflect on the situations and their response to them on their own at home. The second session will also take approximately an hour to complete.

Two sessions outside coaching session (each approximately one hour), followed by some practice time at home.

Session 1

1. Ask your performers to have a brainstorming session on the sort of situations that typically create pressure/stress in their sport. Reinforce that a stressful situation is any situation that is mentally demanding, perhaps important, meaningful and has the capacity to make performers feel uncomfortable, anxious and/or threatened. Emphasise that the situations may occur in training, the pre-competition period, during the competition, after/between competitions. If you are working with a large group of performers, you may wish to divide them into small groups and perhaps focus each on a different category of situation (eg one in training, one pre-competition). Avoid judging any situations generated – brainstorming sessions are about generating individual perceptions without judging their quality.

2. Spend a few minutes discussing the range of situations identified. Then ask the performers to select any two or three of the pressure situations generated in which they performed well (or went on to perform well) and two or three pressure situations in which they performed poorly (or went on to perform poorly).

Selected Pressure Situations When Performed Well	Thoughts	Feelings	Attentional Focus

Then ask the performers to write down and describe their own thoughts, feelings and attentional focus in each of these contrasting scenarios – you may need to give some examples to show what is meant by thoughts, feelings and attentional focus.

Selected Pressure Situations When Performed Poorly	Thoughts	Feelings	Attentional Focus

3 It is important to help performers recognise their unique mental and physical activation state associated with good performance and those associated with poor performance. Avoid any generalisations – encourage performers to use their own words and point out that each performer will have different ideal states. It may be helpful to encourage them to share with each other their experiences of the states that both help and hinder performance. Remember that symptoms such as nervousness, tension, concern and butterflies (signs of somatic and cognitive anxiety) can be positive or negative for different performers. More pertinently, you need to create an atmosphere where performers can talk openly about their states and become more sharply aware of which mental and physical characteristics facilitate rather than debilitate their performances.

4 Encourage them to work on this matrix at home.

Session 2

1 In the next session, encourage the performers to select 10–15 situations they feel are the most important ones they need to handle to perform consistently well. Ask them to write these on the perimeter of the blank profile and for each situation, then rate (out of ten) the extent to which they are able to create an optimal IPS and handle the associated pressure. Tell them to mark these on the profile and ask each to identify the situations with the highest ratings (ie where they handle pressure effectively) and describe the strategies they use to cope with the pressure and achieve their IPS. You may choose to do this follow-up work in a one-to-one situation.

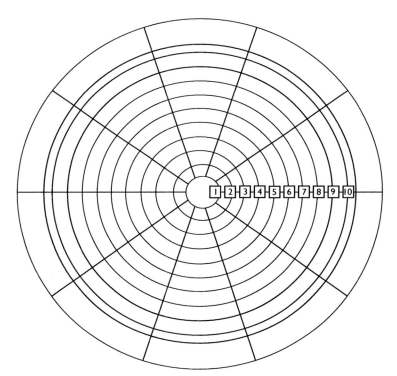

2 This is an ideal time to help your performers understand what happens physically and mentally when they achieve their IPS and when they fail to achieve it. Some explanation of the stress process may be helpful – refer back to Section 1.3 (Page 9). Let them appreciate the different symptoms that occur as a result of stress and different routes that performers can take to cope with those symptoms.

3 Ask the performers to select two sport situations with the lowest ratings for handling pressure (ie where they cannot gain the IPS and fail to cope with the stress). These specific situations may then become the focus of the programme, although the performer's mental and physical responses to other sport situations may be improved as the transferable result of training. You and your performers will now have gained some insight into the areas that need improvement and the type of programme that might be most beneficial to each individual.

It is now suggested that you read through each of the following programmes before engaging in any specific one with your performers. This will not only act as a form of reinforcement but will also allow you to pinpoint more clearly which one(s) may be appropriate, given the fresh and recent insights you have gained for each performer from the exercises in Programme One.

Programme Two: Breathing and Centring

AIM

To help performers achieve their IPS in training and competition by learning to apply the physical relaxation techniques of breathing and centring.

✓ *This programme is particularly beneficial to those performers who associate high levels of somatic anxiety with poor performance (ie negatively) and consequently have difficulty gaining the appropriate physical activation state.*

By the end of this programme, you and your performers should be able to use centring and rhythmic breathing to reduce the symptoms of somatic anxiety and gain a more relaxed physical state in training and competition situations.

Before using this programme, you are recommended to read again the relevant sections on breathing and centring in Section 2.2 (Page 28).

You may wish to choose either rhythmic breathing or centring in Phase A of this programme.

Phase A: Outside the coaching session

Rhythmic breathing

1 Explain to your performers how rhythmic breathing can be a useful technique to help them cope with pressure and so perform better. The amount of explanation you provide will be dependent on the performer (eg age, relevance).

2 Ask your performers to place their hands on the bottom of their rib cage and breathe in deeply (inhale) while you count to three. Encourage them to feel their rib cage expand. Tell them to hold their breath for a count of three and then breathe out (exhale) to the count of three. Repeat a number of times and ask them to notice the effect on their physical and mental state (eg calmer, more focused). If they are used to taking their own pulse, you may encourage them to take it before and after the exercise and note the difference.

Encourage them to experiment with different inhale/hold/exhale ratios (eg in for four, hold for two, out for five); some people may prefer a longer or shorter breathing pattern to gain the relaxation effect. Remember you cannot inhale oxygen fully and effectively unless you have fully exhaled.

3 To help them appreciate how breathing can reduce high levels of physical arousal (associated with somatic anxiety, fatigue, exercise), ask them to carry out some physical activity (eg shuttle running, running up a flight of stairs) to induce mild fatigue and then repeat the deep breathing exercise. Help them to experience how rhythmic breathing can help them recover more quickly and regain their optimal physical state.

You may wish to demonstrate how rhythmic breathing can counter the effect of mental pressure by creating a worry-inducing situation. You will need to be innovative in selecting an anxiety provoking situation such as threatening an immediate fitness test or the requirement for one person to stand up and give a talk to the rest of the group. Once the anxiety response has been evoked, lead them through the rhythmic breathing routine and help them experience how it can alleviate the physical anxiety symptoms experienced.

Ask the performers to suggest the sport situations when they might use the breathing or centring technique. The sort of situations they might choose are listed on Page 30.

4 Encourage them to practise regularly their preferred rhythmic breathing pattern at home (eg while the kettle is boiling, during the adverts on TV), school or work. These moments of practice will aid the conditioning process and make good use of what might be deemed *dead time.*

Centring

1 Explain to your performers how centring can be a useful technique to help them cope with pressure and so perform better. The amount of explanation you provide will be dependent on the performer (eg age, relevance).

2 Demonstrate the centring technique to them (see Page 31) and then lead them through the process several times. Encourage them to try it standing up, sitting down and perhaps in conjunction with a cue word such as *centre, relax* or *focus.*

3 Ask the performers to suggest the sport situations when they might use the breathing or centring technique. The sort of situations they might choose are listed on Page 30.

4 As with rhythmic breathing, encourage them to practise the technique in a variety of situations at home (eg while the kettle is boiling, during the adverts on TV), school or work.

Phase B: Within coaching or training sessions and eventually in competitions

1 Using the situations identified by your performers (and your own experience), try to re-create these situations in training and encourage the performers to adopt their breathing or centring technique. You will probably need to adopt this as a process goal in every training session in the first place. You will also need to be innovative in how you simulate the different situations where a breathing or centring routine can be of benefit. For example, you might devise a penalty competition in training and adopt a pre-penalty routine in which attention is placed on the breathing or centring technique.

2 Initially they will need to be reminded when to use the technique but over time, this should become more self-regulated or even automatic. Eventually it should be used in simulated competitions and then actual competitions. It will be important to monitor how often it is being used and how effectively. Performers might be encouraged to keep a logbook recording when they have employed the technique and its relative success. This could be reviewed with performers each week.

---

1 For further information on different types of goals, you are recommended to the NCF pack *Mental Skills, an introduction for sports coaches,* available from Coachwise Ltd (0113 231 1310).

Programme Three: Progressive Muscular Relaxation

AIM

To help performers achieve their IPS in training and competition through the use of progressive muscular relaxation (PMR) techniques.

✓ *This programme is particularly beneficial to those performers who have difficulty gaining the appropriate physical activation state, particularly those who experience excessive muscle tension indicative of somatic anxiety and associate this with poor performance (ie negatively).*

By the end of this programme, you and your performers should be able to use progressive muscular relaxation (PMR) in three ways:

- As a deep relaxation tool for learning and preparation.
- As a control relaxation tool for pre-competition.
- For the moments requiring composure during performance.

Performers will be able to call on these techniques when they need to release tension and reduce the symptoms of somatic anxiety. Before using this programme, you are recommended to read again the relevant sections on progressive muscular relaxation in Section 2.2 (Page 28).

NB You may wish to develop an audiotape of the instructions for a PMR session
 for control, composure and deep relaxation sessions to give to your performers to practise at home. Alternatively, commercially produced relaxation tapes are readily available.

Phase A: One session outside a coaching session to experience deep relaxation, followed by three weeks individual practice at home

1. Explain to your performers how PMR techniques can be used to help them cope with pressure and so perform better. The amount of explanation you provide will be dependent on the performer (eg age, relevance). Discuss with the performers the kinds of situation in their sport where it is important to possess a relaxed physical state. Distinguish between the use of deep, control and composure relaxation skills which they will learn.

2. Conduct a 15–20 minute relaxation session (deep relaxation) using either a pre-recorded tape or using the script in Activity 8 (Page 33). Remember to ensure a warm and quiet room with few distractions (see guidance on Page 33). Allow time to discuss their experiences and feelings after the session. You may want to do this on more than one occasion.

3. Performers will need to be given an audiotape to practise this technique at home – ideally every day for three weeks. Gradually they should be encouraged to practise the technique without using the tape as a stimulus once they have learnt the sequence and gained some experience. Music might be used to help create the right atmosphere. Monitor their progress and provide appropriate support.

4. During the last week of practice, encourage them to reduce the session from 15 minutes down to about ten. Emphasise that this deep relaxation skill may be useful for general relaxation at home or during the week and evening before an important competition.

Phase B: One session outside a coaching session to learn control relaxation, followed by four weeks individual practice at home

1. Lead a group session based on a ten minute tape/script which would be useful for pre-competition (control) relaxation. Focus on the muscle groups which are used extensively in the sport and therefore the ones more likely to become tense in pressure situations. While tensing and relaxing these particular muscle groups, you might also introduce differential relaxation which involves tensing and relaxing the muscle to differing degrees (eg 50%, 75%, 10%). This would be particularly useful in the specific muscle group(s) where heightened awareness of tension levels is crucial, for example muscles of the forearm for the server in tennis, the quadriceps muscles for the gymnast about to practise the routine on the beam.

2 Encourage performers to practise this control relaxation daily at home for the next three weeks, monitoring and recording progress. Each week they should gradually reduce the session time from ten minutes to six, then to three minutes by the end of the third week. After the first week, encourage the performers to use this form of relaxation immediately after physical training sessions, prior to competition and in other suitable situations. Emphasise that this control relaxation skill is useful in the pre-competition period or during breaks of 10–15 minutes when key muscle groups can be checked and relaxed.

3 During the fourth week, ask performers to focus on spending 30–60 second attention segments on tensing and relaxing single muscle groups which are crucial to performance and in which they tend to experience excessive tension. Encourage this type of composure relaxation to be done 5–10 times per day on a daily basis, in a variety of everyday situations. As well as tension followed by relaxation of the muscle group (active relaxation), performers should now be readily able to relax a specific muscle group (passive relaxation) in response to any observed/unwanted tension.

Phase C: Within the coaching and training session

1 Using the situations identified by the performers (and your own experience), try to re-create these situations in training and encourage the performers to adopt their composure relaxation technique. You will need to adopt this as a process goal in every training session where they practise a 30–60 second relaxation cue isolating the muscle group(s) they want to relax. You will also need to be innovative in how you simulate the different situations where a composure relaxation cue can be of benefit. For example, in tennis you might devise a second serve accuracy competition and suggest a pre-serve routine in which attention is placed on cuing relaxation in the forearm.

2 As with breathing and centring, performers will need to be reminded when to use the technique but over time, this should become more self-regulated and automatic. Having introduced performers to a variety of situations which give them the chance to practise the composure cue, the technique should be employed conscientiously in simulated competitions and then actual competition. It will be important to monitor how often and how effectively it is being used. The performer might be encouraged to keep a logbook, recording when they have employed the technique and its relative success. This could be reviewed with performers each week. In this way, performers will have developed the ability to control muscle tension and induce optimal muscular relaxation in three key scenarios – preparation (deep), pre-competition (control) and during performance (composure).

Programme Four: Meditative and Imagery-based Relaxation

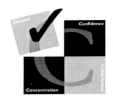

AIM

To help performers achieve their IPS in training and competition through the use of meditative and imagery-based relaxation techniques.

✓ *This programme is particularly beneficial to those performers who have difficulty gaining the appropriate mental activation state – those who experience high levels of cognitive anxiety (eg worry, negative and irrelevant thoughts and images) and associate these with poor performance (ie negatively). The imagery-based relaxation techniques use the same principles and procedures as meditative relaxation, except performers should be encouraged to focus their attention on an image as opposed to a command word. The technique is particularly applicable to those performers whose cognitive anxiety tends to be manifested visually in the form of negative images of failure as opposed to verbally in the form of negative self-talk/doubts. It is important to ascertain whether your performers possess the required imagery skills (vividness and controllability) before they embark on such a programme.*

By the end of this programme, you and your performers should be able to use meditative and imagery-based relaxation techniques to:

- reduce the symptoms of cognitive anxiety
- activate a more positive attentional state. Performers should be able to achieve a positive mental state on three different levels – a deep mental relaxation level for learning and general preparation, an intermediate state of control relaxation for pre-competition and a state of mental composure which can be voluntarily triggered the moment it is required during performance.

Before using this programme, you are recommended to read again the relevant sections on meditative and imagery-based relaxation techniques in Section 2.2 (Page 28).

NB You may wish to develop an audiotape of the instructions for a meditative session for control, composure and deep relaxation sessions to give to your performers to practise at home. Alternatively, commercial tapes can be purchased from reputable companies.

Meditative Relaxation

Phase A: One session outside a coaching session to experience deep relaxation, followed by three weeks individual practice at home

1 Explain to your performers how meditative relaxation can be used to help them cope with pressure and so perform better. The amount of explanation you provide will be dependent on the performer (eg age, relevance). Discuss with the performers the kind of situation where it is important to possess a relaxed and positive mental state, free from negative and/or irrelevant thoughts. Distinguish between the use of deep, control and composure relaxation skills which they will learn in order to activate appropriate attentional states in different situations.

2 Conduct a 15–20 minute meditative relaxation session (deep relaxation) using either a pre-recorded tape or using the script on Page 33. Remember to read the guidelines on Page 33 to increase the effectiveness of the session. Ensure performers have chosen their individual cue word (mantra) and appropriate music has been selected. Allow time to discuss their experiences and feelings after the session. For example, after a period of quietness to relax on their own, did they find themselves much more alert and sensitive to the loudness of the voice? You may want to do this session on more than one occasion.

3 Performers will need to be given an audiotape to practise this technique at home – ideally every day for three weeks. Once they have gained some experience, they should be encouraged to practise the technique without using the tape as a stimulus. Monitor their progress by asking them how effective they were at focusing on the mantra and breathing rhythm. Were they able to refocus when they became distracted?

4 During the last week of practice, encourage them to reduce the session length from 15 minutes down to about ten. Emphasise that this deep relaxation skill may be useful for general relaxation at home, or during the week and evening before an important competition. Encourage performers to attempt a relaxation session in the midst of distractions (eg with the TV on or louder music playing in the other room). This period of training will help performers focus mentally for longer periods on relevant/neutral cues.

Phase B: One session outside a coaching session to learn control relaxation, followed by four weeks individual practice at home

1 Lead a group session based on a ten minute tape/script which would be useful for pre-competition (control) relaxation. The objective of this session is not to take performers into a deep state but to develop their ability to focus the mind consistently on relevant cues for an intermediate period of time.

2 Encourage performers to practise this control relaxation with their chosen mantra daily at home for the next three weeks, monitoring and recording progress. Each week, they should gradually reduce the session length from ten to six minutes, then to three minutes by the end of the third week. After the first week, encourage the performers to use this form of relaxation to refocus attention immediately after physical training sessions, prior to competition and in other adverse situations where there are potential distractions present. Emphasise that this control relaxation technique is useful in the pre-competition period or during breaks of five to ten minutes to help the mind focus or regroup attention on factors relevant to their performance.

3 During the fourth week, ask performers to practise their breathing-mantra sequence for periods of only 30–60 seconds. This exercise will help them develop the skill of activating a positive attentional state in a matter of seconds. Encourage this composure relaxation technique to be repeated five to ten times each day on a daily basis in a variety of everyday situations. Advise performers to switch their focus of attention suddenly from what they were previously thinking/doing to their breathing rhythm and mantra. Under these conditions of mental stress, they will strengthen their ability to refocus quickly on task relevant cues. As some sport skills require mental composure to be achieved within 15 seconds, encourage performers to monitor the time it takes to attend fully to the mantra and clear the mind of previous thoughts. Again, executing this exercise with adverse distractions around serves to insulate the mind more fully.

Phase C: Within the coaching and training session

1 Using the stressful situations identified by your performers (and your own experience), try to recreate these situations in training and encourage performers to adopt their composure relaxation technique. You will need to adopt this as a process goal in every training session where they practise a 15–60 second mental relaxation cue. You will also need to be innovative in how you simulate the different situations where mental composure is a necessity. This is relatively easy to achieve for sports involving time outs or prior to self-paced skills (eg penalties, service games, after scoring a goal). It can also be used during the action, for example when about to receive a pass, having been off the ball.

2 As with breathing and centring, performers will need to be reminded when to use the technique but over time, this should become more self-regulated and automatic. Having introduced performers to a variety of situations which give them the chance to practise the composure cue, the technique should be employed conscientiously in simulated competitions and then actual competition. It will be important to monitor how often it is being used and how effectively. Performers might be encouraged to keep a logbook, recording when they have employed the technique and its relative success. This could be reviewed each week. This will help performers develop the ability to remove worry and negative, irrelevant thoughts in three key situations – general performance preparation (deep), pre-competition (control) and during performance (composure).

Imagery-based Relaxation[1]

Phase A: One session outside a coaching session to experience deep relaxation, followed by three weeks individual practice at home

1 Explain to your performers how imagery-based relaxation can be used to help them cope with pressure and so perform better. The amount of explanation you provide will be dependent on the performer (eg age, relevance). Discuss with your performers the kind of situation in their sport where it is important to possess a relaxed and positive mental state which is free from negative images. Distinguish between the use of deep, control and composure relaxation skills which they will learn in order to activate appropriate images in different situations.

2 Conduct a 15–20 minute imagery-based relaxation session (deep relaxation) using either a pre-recorded tape or using the script on Page 33. Remember to read the guidelines on Page 33 to increase the effectiveness of the session. Allow time to discuss their experiences and feelings after the session. For example, were they able to utilise all their senses within the image? Did they stick to one image or wander to others? Were they able to refocus attention on the image when distracted by the external environment? You may want to do this session on more than one occasion.

3 Performers will need to be given an audiotape to practise this technique at home – ideally every day for three weeks. Gradually they should be encouraged to practise the technique without using the tape. If they wish, they may develop their own imagery script containing images which they find relaxing. Monitor their progress by asking them how effective they were at developing the image, utilising their senses and holding the image within their attention for 10–15 minutes.

4 During the last week of practice, encourage them to reduce the session length from 15 to 10 minutes. Emphasise that this deep relaxation technique may be useful for general relaxation at home or during the week and evening before an important competition. Encourage performers to attempt a relaxation session in the midst of distractions (eg with the TV on or louder music playing in the other room). This training will help performers improve their ability to focus on a meaningful and relaxing image for longer periods.

---

1 For more help on how to introduce and develop imagery techniques, you are recommended to the NCF pack *Imagery Training: a guide for sports coaches and performers*, available from Coachwise Ltd (0113 231 1310).

Phase B: Practising imagery-based control relaxation and confidence building; one session with the coach outside training, followed by three weeks of personal practice

1. Although performers may have their own imagery script which induces relaxation within ten minutes, it may be useful to give them the option of a confidence-building script. With this in mind, lead a session based on a ten minute tape/script which asks performers to recall vividly their best performances in their sport, to rehearse the perfect execution of a skill or to imagine themselves acting confidently in an upcoming competition. Within the ten minutes, you may wish to intersperse relaxing stimuli (eg see yourself coping with the situation by using rhythmic breathing or centring before the start or a restart in the competition) with confidence-building stimuli (eg imaging successful start or restart and the associated feelings of satisfaction).

   This type of positive mental rehearsal or relaxation can be useful to control attention and maximise mental preparation on the night before or just prior to competition. Whether the performers opt for relaxation material or mental rehearsal material, it is important not to take the performer into a deep state. The goal is to condition performers to focus their mind consistently on relevant cues for an intermediate period of time.

2. Encourage performers to practise this form of control relaxation or mental rehearsal daily at home for the next three weeks, monitoring and recording progress. Each week, they should gradually reduce the session length from ten to six minutes, then to three minutes by the end of the third week. After the first week, encourage them to try to switch into their imagery and refocus attention immediately after physical training sessions, prior to competition and in other adverse situations where there are potential distractions. Stress the value of these techniques when used in the pre-competition period or during breaks of five to ten minutes to help focus or regroup attention on factors relevant to their performance.

3. During the fourth week, ask performers to practise a form of instant imagery relaxation or rehearsal for periods lasting only 30–60 seconds. This exercise will help them develop the techniques of activating a positive image state in a matter of seconds. This composure technique should be repeated five to ten times each day on a daily basis, in a variety of everyday situations. Advise performers to switch their focus of attention suddenly from what they were previously thinking/doing to a relaxing or confidence-building image. Ensure that rhythmic breathing accompanies the imagery sequence. Under such testing conditions, performers will strengthen their ability to refocus quickly on relaxing, neutral or task-relevant images. As some sport skills require mental composure to be achieved within 15 seconds, encourage performers to monitor the time it takes them to develop the correct image and clear the mind of previous thoughts/images. Again, executing this exercise with adverse distractions around serves to insulate the mind to a greater degree.

Phase C: Within the coaching and training session

1 Using the stressful situations identified by your performers (and your own experience), try to re-create these situations in training and encourage them to adopt their composure relaxation technique. You will need to adopt this as a process goal in every training session where they practise instantly activating a relaxing or positive rehearsal image. As with other programmes, you will need to be innovative in how you simulate the different situations where mental composure can be achieved via imagery. A good example would be a goalkeeper using 20 seconds of positive imagery (eg looking for the ball and making a clean save) as a form of pre-play just prior to a penalty kick.

2 As with breathing and centring, performers will need to be reminded when to use the technique but over time, this should become more self-regulated and automatic. Having introduced performers to a variety of situations which give them the chance to use imagery for composure and preparation, the technique should be employed conscientiously in simulated competitions and then actual competition. It will be important to monitor how often it is being used and how effectively. Performers might be encouraged to keep a logbook, recording when they have employed the technique and its relative success. This could be reviewed each week. This will help performers develop a buffer against any negative and irrelevant images while countering these with positive images in different phases of mental preparation (ie deep, control, composure).

Programme Five:
Cognitive Restructuring

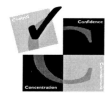

AIM

To help performers use cognitive restructuring techniques to counter negative thoughts and perceptions (eg worry, self-doubt, fear of consequences) about training or competition and gain a more positive attentional focus to enhance performance.

✓ *This programme is particularly beneficial for those performers who have difficulty gaining the appropriate mental activation state or focus – those who engage in negative self-talk which in turn can induce both cognitive and somatic anxiety.*

By the end of this programme, you and your performers should be able to use cognitive restructuring to elicit or maintain a positive and appropriate focus required for optimal performance.

Before using this programme, you are recommended to read again the relevant sections on cognitive restructuring techniques in Section 2.3 (Page 40).

Phase A: Three separate sessions outside normal coaching session (with some parts that might be done at home)

Session 1

1. Explain to your performers how their thoughts can influence their actions and emotions (refer back to Section 2.4, Page 46). You might use the glass being perceived as half full or half empty as an analogy, and the importance of keeping it psychologically as full as possible in all situations. Point out that this attitude is under their own control. You might use some sport-specific examples such as 'how many of you are aware of sometimes thinking something like "I hope I don't serve a double fault" and then serving one, or "I mustn't miss this one" and then missing it?'

2. Ask the performers to have a brainstorming session and write down all the negative or irrelevant thoughts or statements they believe they use in particular sport situations (refer back to Activity 11, Page 42 for examples). Balance this exercise by asking performers to have a brainstorming session of all the positive/relevant thoughts and statements they make within sport situations. Categorise each of these statements into training, pre-competition or during competition periods to ascertain in exactly what situations the performers are most likely to be positive or negative.

	Training	Pre-competition	During Competition
Negative or irrelevant thoughts/ statements			
Positive or relevant thoughts/ statements			

3 For each specific negative statement, encourage them to rephrase it in a positive way. If time is short or to allow greater reflection, you might encourage each performer to complete this exercise at home and bring the list to the next session. You might choose to work individually with performers at the next session or to share answers with the group (if appropriate, letting the group determine who has produced the most positive and meaningful restructured thought).

Session 2

In a second session (or as required), you may test the performers by having a competition to see who is the quickest to react positively. You provide the negative phrase in context and if the performer cannot react immediately with a positive counter statement, he is out of the competition. Continue until you only have one performer left – the most instinctively positive.

Session 3

In the final session, discuss with performers the fact that they may be highly positive but still experience symptoms of somatic anxiety. Encourage them to appreciate they can interpret these symptoms as a sign of a positive state of readiness. Alternatively, if they find the symptoms unpleasant, they can learn how to relax using another technique. Refer back to Activity 12 and/or 5 if they want to practise restructuring or positively interpreting the symptoms of somatic anxiety.

Phase B: During coaching and training sessions over a period of time, eventually using within competitions

For the next few weeks, set a process goal for every training and coaching session in which every performer is charged with verbalising any negative or irrelevant thoughts or feelings experienced. This will help them become more consciously aware of the extent of their negative self-talk and the occasions when it typically seems to happen. As performers identify their negative thoughts within situations, urge them to start the process of thought stopping (eg calling *stop*) and then verbalising positive alternatives out loud. An excellent example of this is to encourage sprinters to verbalise the 20 seconds of positive thoughts they should be having as they go down onto the starting blocks and prepare for the starting gun. The same exercise can be transferred for use before any relatively closed and self-paced skill (eg taking penalties, preparing to start a routine, at a restart, between points in tennis). There is no doubt that a very positive atmosphere can be created in training and simulated competition as performers are set the task of responding positively to any situation that arises. Think of similar examples to use for your sport.

2 Over time, performers will have acquired a whole library of positive statements to use in any situation, particularly those in which they tend to experience cognitive or somatic anxiety. Your goal is to devise as many simulated stressful situations within training so your performers can practise their responses.

Programme Six:
Attitude Management

AIM

To help performers control the way they view potentially stressful situations in training and competition.

✓ *This programme is particularly beneficial for those performers who tend to view stressful situations as outside their control and so experience anxiety.*

By the end of this programme, you and your performers should be able to control the way they approach difficult or pressure situations by developing an attitude that focuses on the things that can be controlled (ie the process) rather than the outcomes which cannot be controlled.

Before using this programme, you are recommended to read again the relevant sections on attitude management in Section 2.4 (Page 46).

Phase A: Outside a coaching session

☐ Explain to your performers the importance of learning to control anything that can be controlled, of learning to manage their own attitude and approach towards anxiety provoking situations. Work through Activity 13 (Page 47) with your performers. Ask them to:

- explain what achievement in sport means to them
- identify the components which determine whether or not they achieve
- categorise these components into factors (eg technical, physical)
- mark the components/skills that can be controlled (ie for which the performer is responsible)
- assess the relative importance of these controllable components/skills to the eventual outcome
- decide what they should be focusing on in competition.

Components	Factors	Controllable	Importance

Focus on:

2 Reinforce how success in outcome terms can only be managed by focusing on the controllable factors – usually those associated with personal performance. Use a relevant example from your sport (eg the penalty taker) and describe how she could view the stressor in either an uncontrollable or controllable manner. This should lead to a discussion about the importance of setting process goals in training and competition. It is important to reinforce this repeatedly and consistently over the next few months.

Phase B: Outside coaching session (one hour approximately)

1 Reinforce the fact that in any stressful situation, it is important to focus on the things that can be controlled and focus on performance and process goals. Ask the performers to brainstorm on *what if?* situations – situations they have experienced or can think of which are potentially anxiety provoking. Refer back to Page 50 if you need some examples as prompts to help them get started.

What if?	Contingency Response
'I've got to score a 9.5 to win the competition'	*Let the work you've put in dictate how well you do. You can only be as good as your best effort*

2 For each one, work through and agree how each situation could be managed. Keep them focused on the factors they can control and help them adopt the attitude of letting go of the things outside their control.

3 You may encourage performers to practise verbalising their controllable responses to the stressor in training. For example, prior to taking a penalty, a centre-forward might say 'It's about taking a clean penalty and placing it in the top right-hand corner' as opposed to 'This has got to go in somehow or else we're history!' You will need to reinforce appropriate *what ifs?* repeatedly in training and use the exercise before important competitions to deal with specific issues that might arise.

Programme Seven: Mental and Physical Activation

Phase A: Within a coaching session (1–2 hours) followed by 1–2 weeks of awareness work

NB Although part of this session involves the coach providing explanation and education, there is a high component of demonstration which could be facilitated at the training site (eg pitch, court, track).

▯ Explain to performers the importance of creating the optimal mental (ie alert, interested, focused) and physical (ie energised, pumped, emotionally up) activation states. Emphasise that, in some cases, handling pressure means increasing their arousal levels so they are activated appropriately for the task. Ask performers to list any methods they use or can think of which would increase their mental and physical arousal levels. Refer back to Section 2.5 (Page 51) for further ideas.

2 Discuss when they might use these methods – night before, immediately pre-competition, during performance. Determine whether your performers really use these techniques regularly and consider whether you create the coaching environment to foster their use.

3 Ask one performer to try to increase her mental and physical arousal levels by repeatedly taking very short, sharp and shallow breaths. Ask the other performers to watch carefully and suggest any other actions that might be taken (eg tightly closing eyes and focusing on selected images, picturing anger, making the breathing noisy and more staccato, using positive self-talk to pump self up, clenching muscles and fists). Without judging the use of these additional tools that may come naturally, ask performers to try the breathing technique and then accompany this with anything that naturally increases their arousal.

You may find that this type of breathing on its own is not sufficient to evoke a highly mentally and physically activated response. It is important, therefore, to reinforce to performers that increasing simple biological or physiological activation can be done by quick breathing, short vigorous activity (eg shuttle running) or perhaps muscle tensing and literally squeezing the body. However, this does not directly activate the more emotional and mental aspects of arousal.

4 Suggest to performers three other key tools which might also charge emotion and increase alertness and interest in the task: imagery, music and self-talk. Spend some time on the following three activities.

Ask performers to consider what they would choose to image if they wanted to get emotionally charged, even positively angry. Typical examples might be:

- their best sporting moments, recalling emotional events in their life
- running the final leg of a race with the crowd going wild
- a scene/sequence from a film which provokes emotions of anger, aggression or excitement (eg *Braveheart* or *Legends of the Fall* where Brad Pitt's wife is killed with a ricochet bullet)
- the opposition
- achieving their goals.

5 Encourage them to experiment with their various pieces of emotional imagery in the next two weeks at home and/or at training.

6 Ask performers to consider the type of music that sparks their emotion and alertness (psych-up music). Ask them to share examples of favourite songs that really get them going. Generally this music will have a strong melody, fast tempo and major harmony (eg *Eye of the Tiger*) if it stimulates confidence-related emotions. However, songs with a slower tempo can also provide powerful emotion (eg Celine Dion's title song from *Titanic*) because of their significance. Encourage performers to record their favourite emotional pieces of music for use on a Walkman while out running or as part of a pre-competition preparation routine.

7 Ask performers to consider what phrases they might use to get themselves fully engaged in the task and emotionally ready to compete. You might prompt by suggesting or demonstrating the three types of self-talk: importance-talk, personal-talk and confrontational talk (refer back to Section 2.5, Page 51 for examples). You might also like to show extracts of motivational psych-up talks from the documentary video about the 1997 British Lions tour to South Africa. You might encourage performers to verbalise their positive intentions to training partners by telling them what they are going to do to them or their opponents, for example 'I hope you're ready to get absolutely nailed. Have you ever experienced one of my tackles? There's one coming soon. You're facing a real problem – me.'

8 Ask the performers to select techniques they can test in training and use ultimately in the build-up to competition and during performance. Ask them to think of how training might be structured to allow them to experiment with their emotions.

Phase B: Within coaching and training sessions

1 You will need to be innovative about ways to integrate this work into actual coaching and training sessions for it will depend very much on the sport. Refer back to Section 2.5 (Page 51) for further examples. Some of these activities may be difficult and time-consuming to use. The key is to find ways to help your performers identify their ideal mental and physical activation states and then be able to practise expressing them.

Final Summary

By working through this pack, you will have been introduced to the theoretical and practical issues involved in handling pressure in competitive sport. As coaches, you should now be able to appreciate the size and complexity of the topic and realise that this pack is just the beginning. Sport psychologists tend to agree that the key to handling pressure is to develop three critical psychological skills in your performers:

- They must have the right **motivational attitude** and approach to competition. If they have poor attitude management and their motives are too extrinsic and uncontrollable, they will not only feel pressure but they are less likely to handle it effectively. Performers must have a rational and intrinsic perspective to winning, losing and personal performance levels. Good luck to any coach whose performers repeatedly lack that fundamental mental skill.

- They must have cast iron **attentional control** which reflects the performers' ability to fill their minds with positive and task-relevant thoughts in any situation in which they find themselves. This is common sense to most coaches but rarely does their coaching actually allow performers to practise positive attentional control. If they do not practise how to fill their minds with positive thoughts, the pressure of competition will do an effective job of filling the empty space with negative thoughts (ie cognitive anxiety).

- They need to have complete **control** over their **emotions.** The physical activation state of a performer can be the difference between coming first or last in a race; winning Wimbledon or throwing a 4–1 lead. Sport demands technical and physical skills which can suffer if the machine is overheating, too stiff or too cold. Rather than allow the pressure of competition to dictate the emotional status of the performer, the performer needs to dictate how he wants to feel and when. Your coaching practice must allow for emotional experimentation to be structured in training. This is alongside some of the reactive techniques (eg relaxation) which are important in reacting to the stress if it has already controlled the performer's state.

The seven programmes in this pack have offered some practical insights into how these three skills can be developed. Now comes the test – to apply this knowledge regularly and systematically to your coaching practice. Good luck!

You may now wish to work through other packs[1]:

*Butler, R (1996) **Performance profiling** (audiotape and book) Leeds, National Coaching Foundation. ISBN 0-947850-36-8

* Hale, B (1998) **Imagery training: a guide for sports coaches and performers.** Leeds, National Coaching Foundation. ISBN

Hardy, L, Jones, G and Gould, D (1996) **Understanding psychological preparation for sport: theory and practice.** Chichester, Wiley. ISBN 0-471-95787-9

* Maynard, I (1998) **Improving concentration.** Leeds, National Coaching Foundation. ISBN 1-902523-01-6

* Morris, T (1997) **Psychological skills training in sport.** Leeds, National Coaching Foundation. ISBN 0-947850-78-3

* Sellars, C (1997) **Building self-confidence.** Leeds, National Coaching Foundation. ISBN 0-947850-34-1

* Available from Coachwise Ltd (0113 231 1310).

Explanation of Key Terms

Activation (Page 13) refers to the physical and mental state of readiness of an individual.

Anxiety (Page 15) occurs if the individual appraises a stressor to be potentially threatening. It can be:

- **cognitive** (mental) which is characterised by such things as fear of failure, negative expectations, worry and self-doubt
- **somatic** (physical) which is characterised by physical symptoms such as nausea, increased heart rate or muscle tension.

Cognitive Appraisal (Page 14) is the process through which the individual weighs up the demands imposed by the stressor.

Goal-setting is a way of establishing objectives and providing direction. Different types of goals can be identified such as:

- **outcome goal** which refers to the type which describes a particular outcome or end result (eg winning, gaining selection) and are not therefore totally under the control of the performer
- **process** or performance goals which refer to the process or way the individual wishes to perform (eg achieving a particular time or distance, the number of successful tackles or unforced errors) and are therefore more readily under the control of the individual.

Ideal Performance State (IPS) refers to the specific mental and physical activation state needed by an individual for optimal performance of a particular skill.

Mental Qualities (Section 1.1, Page 1) refer to the mental factors that contribute significantly to learning new skills and producing consistent high level performance (eg the 4Cs: commitment, concentration, confidence and control).

Mental Training Techniques (Section 1.2, Page 6) refer to methods used to cope with difficult situations in sport and life in general (eg goal-setting, imagery, positive self-talk).

Stress (Page 14) is a process initiated when the brain interprets an internal or external stimulus as potentially threatening or damaging to the individual (physically or psychologically).

Stressor (Page 14) is any form of external (eg noise, light) or internal (eg thought, image) picked up the individual